Your Divine Power Within

Your Divine Power Within

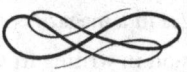

Cultivate Self Awareness, Healing and Wisdom

Zoey Bullock

For your journey,
This book is dedicated to your ascension.
May you experience love and joy in all forms.
This is a space to tune into the divine sprit within,
So you can experience the totality of creation.
This is an activation.
Connecting you with your highest self.
Cultivating awareness.
Taking action in alignment with source.
To live in the beauty of All That Is.
You are infinite by design.

Table of Contents

Acknowledgements

I am deeply grateful to share these transmissions and the beauty of All That Is. I'd like to acknowledge and thank everyone who has been a part of this beautiful journey.

Thank you to my parents for their unwavering love throughout my life, even in the darkest moments I was held by the support and encouragement of my bloodline. The lessons of love have been invaluable, knowing that you always had faith in me.

To my mother, your strength inspires me and I've learned so much from seeing your journey unfold in harmony. May you always experience the bountiful love you deserve.

Special thanks to my ancestors and the spirits who've already transitioned, those who have left powerful imprints on this earth. I carry your presence with me in every moment as I share these words.

To my father, I know that you are experiencing the peace you've always dreamed of. It was an amazing path to show you the healing power within, and I still carry your spirit with me.

To my children, you are the light that forever shifted my path into love and self discovery. I'm overflowing with love as I raise the future generation of inspirational leaders and artists.

To my community, I am honored that we continue to do this work and help others remember the truth within. As we grow, I will continue to be a selfless servant in this walk of life. I would like to express my sincere gratitude for Venus and how you've been so welcoming and held space for so many to heal.

To my readers, thank you for your support. I'm especially thankful to those who were patiently waiting for this book release as the publishing process has been a journey in itself. Your feedback and encouragement have inspired me to continue writing and sharing these channeled messages with you. I admire your willingness to open your hearts to these messages and trust that you hold the keys to your personal transformation.

I offer my profound thanks to the source that flows through all things, guiding and inspiring us towards greater understanding, love and compassion. I'm honored to share these transmissions with the hope to deepen your connection and intuitive wisdom.

Lastly, I want to acknowledge the infinite power of the Universe and the divine forces that continue to guide me. I am grateful for the lessons and miracles that have led me to this moment, as I trust the unfolding of this new earth.

With love and gratitude,

Zoey Bullock

Chapter 1
The Origin of Separation

The transmission is here. I am here to activate your inner wisdom and help you to understand the divine power you possess.

There is no need to experience or hold onto negative feelings. We are all created as pure love and endless joy; only the conditioning from society has disconnected us from this source of connection and higher consciousness.

You are here to experience this activation. You've found this book to journey deeper into the godliness and truth within. There is no coincidence, only synchronicity, and alignment. Here and Now.

Start reading this book from a place of gratitude that your divinity is unfolding and working for you, and the miracles will only continue to amplify in every moment. I've received these transmissions from the archangels to activate the remembrance within you.

I am not here to paint a picture of constant bliss because we live in a world full of collusion and influence. However, I encourage you to take seriously the importance of distinguishing what is in your highest good or, as I like to call it, "guardian angel" self and what merely appears to be a positive influence.

You will learn how to tune into your source of truth within, where alignment is discovered through decisions centered on wholeness and divinity. This book series will reconnect you with your power so you can act from a place of significance to the God within versus external distraction.

Through this activation, you will cultivate an awareness of new situations and decisions meant for alignment versus what is not in your highest good.

You've been drawn to this book to accelerate your ascension journey and tap into the truth within, as the clarity you seek exists inside your vessel already. This source of divine intelligence is within you. This voice is heard and felt inside the knowingness of your soul. I am here to guide you in tapping into that truth.

The clarity you seek exists not in your ability to see or pay attention to my words as you read this book but in your commitment to surrendering. Let go of all the beliefs that have given you a perception or mindset based on pain, struggle, or ego so that you can access what you desire in life.

I am unveiling the natural ways to come to a deeper understanding of your inner wisdom and to see life from the lens of pure potentiality.

You are an infinite connection to God, as this source exists within you to truly grasp the nature of your spiritual ascension. By allowing yourself to feel and experience this power, your life will transform infinitely. Instead of searching for purpose or direction, you will be led by your internal guidance. Through these words, I am speaking life into your journey so you can follow the path to freedom and expansion.

Regardless of your current experience, start this journey focusing on seeing every moment as a chance to deepen your knowledge and grow spiritually, which will dramatically shift your path forward. So today, commit to this journey and allow yourself to be guided.

This book has been channeled through the voice of my ancestors to bring quantum expansion to your spiritual journey. You are your best source of information and light, but reading these words takes you into the very presence needed to find that light. Guiding you into this transmission to ignite your own godliness and innate power.

Pay attention to themes that may seem repetitive or triggering, to trust that these are reminders to embed those uncomfortable lessons in the ascension process. This is about letting go and surrendering to access the pure magic inside.

In the present moment, I am here to align you with the truth inside so you can live in a state of freedom. To find the constant flow of divine guidance and higher intelligence, where life experience is bliss. Because it is your birthright to embody power, joy, and fulfillment.

Are you feeling called to action in this current reality? It is time to shift within yourself to know the depths of truth, heal yourself, and bring new levels of healing to this earth.

If leading a life full of toxins and negative energy, the resulting choices are often not in service to our consciousness. Many of the limits you've experienced originate from the frequencies we bring into existence. What are you welcoming that is not aligned with your highest good?

To reach the levels of joy and freedom that you desire, there are many things for you to remember. First, the illusion of separation has been the conditioning you've experienced for many generations and even in past lives, which has disconnected you from the birthright of your limitless self. Reclaiming that self-sovereignty is a long path of awareness, acknowledgment, and releasing what is keeping you from that power.

Instead of perpetuating the same cycles of behavior that have led you into more fear and anxiety, you are precisely where you need to be to reclaim that personal power.

Now you will understand the multifaceted nature of reality and the actual capabilities that you possess. To this point, your understanding of such may have been insufficient to no fault of your own or the path thus far. Trust that I am your guide to new depths of life and understanding of divinity.

As the goddess of love and enlightenment, I've come to share this gift of the new world to help you understand your infinite potential on this earth. But unfortunately, humans have been led into a realm of confusion where our thoughts are subject to the media's influence, conditioning from our upbringing, and many other external factors.

You've come here to remember the truth cultivated from the source inside. This is where you meet the wholeness and entirety of constant connection. Soon, you will understand how to utilize this knowledge for personal growth and ascension. Because as you ascend, the lower vibrational feelings and patterns will be released to create space for expansion.

This is an invitation to look inward and ask yourself the more difficult questions of why you seek external things to solve for clarity in your life. To go within is to find the direction and authentic source of guidance. This invitation will bring your attention to a new perspective where all those challenges are solved simply by placing the trust back within yourself.

At six years old, I remember putting on a tie-dye T-shirt, sun shades, and dozens of brightly colored bead necklaces. Back then, I wanted to help everyone experience freedom and world peace. The same goal has been carried through my adulthood, where I've spent many years cultivating my knowledge of different natural healing and consciousness expansion modalities.

Seeing firsthand my own source of divinity has kept me on this path, which has led me to continue releasing old cycles of thinking and behavior. To now teach others how to end the cycle of trauma and access their highest self.

Earlier in the journey, I wasn't aware of how or why I was harboring and feeding such feelings, essentially keeping myself and those feelings trapped in my subconscious. So rather than working through the pain and seeking awareness, I buried them deeper into numbing, dissociation, and procrastination patterns.

Outsiders would view me as successful in life, but inside I was perpetuating cycles of pain. The only way to release that was to fully surrender those thoughts and be in my purest essence. Sometimes spiritual bypassing can look like freedom or abundance, but inside, you are disconnected from yourself and your spirit.

Coming to many moments of self-realization, I slowly found my way back to remembrance of my true self. This is where I embraced a deeper understanding of my true power and how to help others embody their gifts.

The activations in this book series are transmissions meant to bring clarity and inspire you to tune into your own divinity and trust that everything is working for your highest good.

This is not a place where I share my journey, nor for me to attempt to prescribe a path for you to follow. I am giving you this activation to remember your true self and find the wholeness and truth that have always been within. Please download the audio version of this book because my voice is a vibrational shift and activation for you to come back into your complete and authentic presence.

From a physical sense, it may seem like you are limited by what you can see. However, this is only one form of reality, as we are all multi-dimensional beings. The actual process of ascension is about reaching a higher vibrational frequency, and in doing so, we find the experience of pure love and joy. The happiness we all seek is simply the alignment of our purpose and the collective unity of All That Is.

Throughout this journey, I will help you cultivate an awareness of what is meant by All That Is and how you are connected inside to the infinite source of consciousness. You are opening to new possibilities that welcome more peace and abundance.

As you read my words, you access a deeper vibration of peace, feeling the energy transmission and allowing yourself to receive. Challenges and resistance arise when internal self-belief is lacking. Simplicity is found when you are constantly trusting the channel of truth within.

If you are faced with unfavorable circumstances that aren't aligned with your true nature, take the time to internalize that thought process and see where your energetic attachments may have led you astray. Think of this book as a reminder and guide back to this channel of truth and light inside your spirit.

Resistance happens when there is mistrust of the soul. Aligning and receiving take place when you are fully open to all possibilities. It follows the principles of energy reciprocation; when you place the intention into the universe, it is returned as such.

Remember that your thoughts influence your vibration when you feel tired, rundown, or overwhelmed. The more you have conscious awareness of those thoughts, the easier it is to change the negative feelings associated that may try to invade or distract you from your purpose.

By studying the philosophy of alchemy as it pertains to our everyday living, we find that happiness is characterized as the point of ultimate expansion. This point is achieved when the human body is freed from the perceived limits of existence and arrives at an internal point of active intelligence. I call this the connection to divine intelligence, where access to the source is constantly flowing.

It's not that you work to achieve these zero points but that you learn how to keep utilizing and expanding this connection as a natural state of existence. It is not about opening the door to the divine because it is already open.

You are simply accessing your own unique connection or stream of such information. Learn to see beneath the noise and external inputs that do not belong to you.

It is not enough to want to see through your third eye but beyond what you'd see physically to the vibrational frequency at which you operate. The peace in your soul. To vibrate at a level of bliss where you are not concerned or threatened by anything that may or may not happen around you.

The ability to feel nourished in all moments, without any substance or external comforts. To be aware of your state of consciousness to shift and quantum leap into your dreams. Using tools such as the breath and earth elements to remind you of the godliness within.

When you keep stagnating or not making progress on specific goals, the comfort you feel is addicting. Realize that the comfort you find in others can easily be misleading or confusing when you are not centered within yourself. To accelerate quickly without fear or doubt, you must learn to trust the messaging that originates from you and your connection to spirit.

Beyond your own spiritual connection, we are all connected. While it is meant for you to experience all levels of relationships, nothing in those external conditions should influence your energy field. If the spirits of others are continuing to pull at you, that is where the power and personal sovereignty need to be reclaimed.

Assert that these external things and people have no control over you. Nothing meant for you in divine light will need any convincing or grandeur attempts to influence. On the contrary, it will enter with ease and alignment to uplift you so you can flourish in your energy and the union and connections you manifest.

You are already full, so you are attracting new situations based on the wholeness of your being. Anything you draw towards you as new will overflow with pure love and abundance rather than drain your energy.

There is no value in placing extended trust in the outside world because much of it was constructed to take attention away from your divinity.

I am here to bring you back to the purest form of yourself. For you to develop a new perspective based on principles of trust in your mind, body, and soul. To give you the step-by-step path would not be valuable; instead, the goal is to prepare you to find that power yourself.

Holistic empowerment lies in the ability to access your channel of light in every moment. Not just occasional gut feelings but the assurance that is received in the constant knowingness.

When you are in that place of home in you, everything will move forward for your highest good. The source inside and what you hold deep within that root dictates what you attract, especially regarding other people.

The discernment of where the energy is focused is the protection against what doesn't serve you. Beyond that is where and to whom you are divinely guided. Lean into intuition as a decision-making tool, even when the push is deep into uncharted waters. Try to view that extra push as excitement rather than fear of things not going as planned. You wouldn't feel strongly called to this action if it wasn't meant for your acceleration and embodiment.

There is no feeling of fear, lack, or doubt when you are rooted in your power. No amount of yoga, breathwork, meditation, ice baths, ceremonies, journaling, or whatever the tool may be will complete or bring fulfillment as the wholeness already exists within. While these practices are helpful, the true self in its purest form is the miracle. Don't ignore that depth within yourself by focusing on what is happening around you.

There is nothing outside of that inner self that you really need to reach completion. Evolution happens when you stop searching or wanting answers to solve your problems. This is when you realize that everything you've been searching for is nowhere to be found and that the only solution is to look at your reflection first and see the love inside.

This love is here now, within your purest essence. There is nothing to search for, nothing to see, and no confusion to settle for because your existence alone is a gift of higher consciousness.

Chapter 2
Connection to the Divine

You are the connection to the divine. The portal to your highest self exists in the here and now. As you rise into this expansive space, you step into the fullness of your light.

The existence you've known in this 3-dimensional reality is only one aspect of the unity consciousness of All That Is. This is where energy flows freely, and you can navigate the universe without feeling any lack or restriction.

Everything you want to experience is connected to you already. Embody that feeling, and it opens the portal to elevation and higher consciousness. With the narrow focus, you feel the bliss instead of the spiritual warfare.

The only thing holding you back from that bliss was the beliefs and holding onto "something else" when you just needed to let go. Focus on the release, the surrender to be within. You will be in your own presence in all of its radiance and love because we are all made of that pure love. That is really the highest level of ascension and connection to source. Remember that love.

The universe brought you here for healing so you can feel that power within. Feeling that connection to yourself and nature will spark the path forward. The actual value in messages from this book and your own downloads or meditations is in the integration and how you continue to do the work. As you receive this transmission, you've already started to resonate at a higher frequency.

While writing this book, I was tempted to share the depths of my journey. But I learned along the path that it would be more meaningful to speak light into your channel and share the activations that I've been so grateful to receive. That being said, these words will align with your growth and bring you into a unified state of consciousness.

This is the space where you will receive the miracles and lessons you are meant to experience, with a deeply rooted connection to your source of power.

Stories of the past only deliver repeated patterns or trigger your own memories. This transmission has come into your realm for a more significant reason that will be revealed over time as you sit with the concepts you read here and apply them to your ascension process. To expand in the present moment, transcending limiting places of fear and pain.

You've come to access the infinite depth beneath the surface with your connection to divine intelligence. To see the world for

All That Is and to feel the movement of energy as you raise your vibration and access this truth.

Throughout this activation, you will experience the universe's nature for healing, expansion, and creation. I will refer to source as you, and you are connected to the source of this overflowing love. Understanding this concept will renew your sense of inspiration and creativity into a new world where you are meant to access this power.

Regardless of your beliefs before this book, keep an open mind from the perspective of trusting your divine path.

Instead of attaching to ideals created by societal structures driven by television, social media, or other sources of influence, you will learn to connect to the trust within you; and know that you are enough. There is no lack, doubt or negativity when you are tuned into yourself in the present moment.

The reality is that there is nothing material outside of yourself that will lead to true fulfillment. It is the experience of freedom that we strive for. While freedom can be created through monetary conditions, the concept of abundance is simply living in overflow and experiencing love in all parts of your essence.

What if the entire concept of life and human responsibility you've grown to believe is not the whole picture? When we go deeper to question the validity of the conditioning we've experienced, the illusions of separation fall quickly.

Distractions in your physical reality will continue if you feed attention to external validations rather than prioritizing the power within. The internal presence expands through stillness, where things like technology may feel like a constant gravitational pull.

The intent of societal structures has been to disconnect you from the most trustworthy source of connection within. By consciously choosing to turn inward, the interconnectedness of All That Is becomes unavoidable.

When grounding into the present moment, the realization contained in these transmissions becomes simple. That view of separation is what leads to all of our troubles and sickness. This separation we've been taught unconsciously holds us in a place of fear and emotional reactivity. Not being able to release such pain in a healthy, natural way only compounds the feeling of stagnancy.

There comes the point where your focus needs to be strong, where nothing can impede it. Obstacles will be present. In fact, more obstacles may arise as you ascend into new vibrations. Until you are in a state of true self-mastery, there may be wavering in your steps when challenges arise. The current human nature, where we've learned to suppress our feelings and internalize emotions, is not the natural state of being.

Many of us have been conditioned from a very young age to view ourselves as separate from our desires. This illusion of separation is what keeps us from achieving those dreams. But it is simply that, an illusion. Your heart wants these possibilities because they are already underway in this present reality. The path to those dreams is as simple as connecting to your inner power.

If you perceive yourself as struggling, you will continue living in a world full of conflict and suffering. No one inherently wants to live in cycles, yet you've found yourself time after time in toxic situations or behaviors.

It is not a matter of getting rid of anything in the way of those desires, as nothing is in the way. Instead, the illusion of separation keeps us worrying about our external conditions, where the true importance lies in how we manage our energy. The illusion keeps you thinking that you are hurting or struggling when the physical body was never designed to hold onto or bury pain, emotion, or worry.

Instead of thinking about where you are in the current physical realm, the focus is shifted to how you can influence your energy field. When you can see how the inner world manifests such miracles around you, the focus will remain there inside. The godliness is your pure form and of much more excitement than any person or place could promise toward your ascension.

If the attention is constantly placed outside, the interruptions take the focus away from your source messaging to the flimsy manipulation from other beings. Take yourself more seriously to prioritize that alignment versus constantly being swayed by the external world pulling your attention.

When distraction is present, we allow that input to penetrate our path instead of strengthening our internal focus. We are tested to show how we can remain consistent and not be swayed by temptation.

You are meant to feel what you are going through in every moment. Not for suffering or to silence your voice but to glow to a greater awakening of light. The traumas and the troubles have gifted you with lessons of growth and divinity.

Understanding the forces of nature support this transformation, but only by being aware of the depths of the darkness first. You are here to understand all of yourself, not just the pleasurable and glorious parts.

Your light can only shine bright when you can see inside the depths of your shadows. Avoiding these feelings will only delay and deepen the pain you experience. Rather than seeking drugs, sex, shopping, or whatever the numbing mechanism may be, start thinking about the expected growth when you feel yourself slipping into that black hole.

What is the feeling you are running from with these escapes? Because I guarantee that rising above that experience will feel much better than whatever crutch you've been seeking for that temporary joy.

You've experienced some degree of pain, grief, or trauma. Healing and growth mean allowing the soul to see into that perception of difficulty and feel every part of it. Not to pretend that life is only love and light because it is not the light that will save you from your shadow behaviors. Instead, it is about illuminating your light in the darkness and understanding all parts of yourself and your experiences.

Anytime you've experienced pain or trauma, your belief system is what classified those memories as unfavorable. Healing and growth allow the soul to feel and see the darkness but to realize, regardless of the perception, that there is love to find in all.

Furthermore, releasing the shadows is much easier if you continue to resonate on the frequency that you can send love, even in the most challenging circumstances.

How would there be a way to rise above your bullshit if you can't even face what is bringing you down. This is not a calling to relive or recall those memories, but to know what the suffering is so you can choose not to suffer anymore.

The human tendency may be to bury or suppress those feelings, but if the root of that feeling is avoided, how can you ever expect to stop feeling the weight of it?

If the absolute truth is that there is no suffering and it is just a place of fear you put yourself mentally, then there is inherently no reason to run from it because it would be bypassing the true love and compassion within.

Feel into your authentic self rather than attempting to leave yourself to find answers or fulfillment. If you were taught to avoid suffering, you've essentially been removed from the compassion and truth within. This is where fear comes from when you associate the potentiality of the future with worry or concern that you will get hurt or experience adversity.

If you don't want to remain where you are, stop yourself from succumbing to the comfort. This is the time to connect with your desires and push yourself to be uncomfortable where it matters.

This means that if there is something that you want, instead of seeing it as a dream, feel into where the growth and manifestation can quickly occur. All of the changes you make will be a change in perspective. Changes that will bring you closer to your true natural power.

There is no responsibility to bear for others. Even when those are dependents of ours; children, partners, parents. The universe supports the needs of those relationships, which often are a mirror to reflect emotion. In the absence of those fear-based emotions, the realization is there is no control over the outcome. Refusing the need for control means trusting and having faith in All That Is. Even when your surroundings are unfavorable.

Stress about the past or the future is meaningless when those particles are interchangeable. If all events occur simultaneously, no root cause for worry is present. It is simply a matter of understanding the truth. To allow things to be as they are and focus on the internal state of being.

You are already connected to the destiny that is soulfully your birthright. It is yours, embedded within your spiritual DNA. Your existence is purposeful, and connecting deeper into that presence will bring alignment and simplicity to the path forward.

The mindset that supports your transformation is one of awareness that you are a force of love and creation. Everything within you is connected to the source. Therefore, feeling through the lower vibration energy is necessary to release the patterning embedded in your life path. This is neither selfish nor self-serving to prioritize releasing what no longer serves you.

When you learn not to settle, it is not necessarily about who or what you are surrounded by. It is your willpower. If a particular presence is triggering, come to a resolution by detaching the need for control over the circumstances. The only person you have control over is yourself.

Trust that the cast of characters engaged in your life is meant to reveal lessons rather than to cause you distress or be the "source" of your happiness. Always think of what is being reflected or why you are triggered. Release that attachment to worry and fear.

"I trust the source within. If that trust wavers, I'm allowing my focus to shift from the present moment."

As you receive this transmission, you will act from a place of awareness rather than reaction. You will be empowered to give up comfort and move toward what you truly want. The boundaries of society do not exist when we are connected to our souls— physical matter containing the infinite spirit of creation.

Chapter 3
Pure Essence

Your life experience is supported by the guides you give essence, from which your breath emerges. The purest form of authenticity supports the divine alchemy of human experience.

You discover true existence by knowing the world within yourself and not by searching for yourself in the world. Rather than projecting your illusion externally, you find the power inside.

The foundational work begins with accessing divine intelligence as a tool for evolution. This occurs without substance, in a moment of silence, where you hold your mind in a place of emptiness and allow yourself to receive because your connection is continually expanding.

Everyone possesses an innate ability to use this guidance, and ignoring that will often lead to disarray. The world is designed to bring us new layers of confusion. To find clarity, we should be grateful in all moments and allow the vibrational energy to do all the work for us.

There is nothing you need to change within yourself because the universe supports exactly who you are now and who you are becoming. The path to embodying your true essence involves letting go of the shame to feel the activation of your purpose. To find that home within you.

The channel between us and the divine is an interconnected web of curiosity, growth, and transcendence into a new level of peace. If the focus of life were purely to obtain abundance, we would need more substance to understand ourselves and our desires.

In reconnecting with your truth, the weight of emotion and the cycles you perpetuate will be lifted from your shoulders. Instead of seeing yourself as the victim, where life is happening to you, you are connecting your spirit to the wisdom that exists in the stillness.

And in the true simplicity of All That Is, you find yourself. The search becomes an internal quest rather than one of disconnection and searching outside of yourself for validation.

You will find that the more you shift within, the universe will continue to test your understanding. This could appear as challenges with boundaries or other triggering lessons. Almost like the flow of action mirrors your karmic imprinting, where cycles from past lives or your ancestors appear in your present timeline. Moving forward in divinity means listening to that God within and not repeating behaviors or beliefs that don't belong to you.

The only way to create sustainable change is to know yourself beyond the past, beyond your interpretation of what is possible, and lastly, to know your personal connection to the oneness that is.

In the vast nothingness, you surrender to the flow. The realization emerges as you consciously decide to be a part of this ascension. This transformation comes in due time when you eliminate the fear and conflict held within.

We strive for control over our circumstances, to work, love, spend time, and learn. But when too much attention is attached to the doing and achieving of future possibilities, our mind shifts away from the beauty existing in the present.

In far too many moments, our mind is pushing or pulling. Think of it this way. If we are concerned with the future outcome of a situation, we are pushing too much value on the future. Or when we constantly recall past cycles, we are pulling.

While motivation and endurance typically are positive attributes, dwelling on the past or anticipating the future requires our minds to perceive it as separate from the Here and Now.

The same is valid for pulling, in which case, we are pulling up old memories or past circumstances, which shift our present vibration.

When we remain in a state of being, there is no value attached to the past or present; the only option that remains is to be; to be in love and gratitude. By allowing yourself simply "to be," your conditioning shifts from "I want" or "I remember" to a full-hearted "I am."

Signs will come to show you the way. In the light, there exists an unwavering commitment to your personal transformation. The power of creation speaks directly through your soul. These words are here to bring you back to that.

Your day-to-day life will change vibrationally, and instead of viewing yourself as separate, you will understand the interconnectedness of All that Is. The hope can be for an overnight transformation, but just as these traumas and barriers accumulate over time, you must trust that the miracles will appear as often as you open yourself to receive them. Trust the process.

The concept of God speed comes into play when you access the forces of creation within yourself. This activation is the transcendence from your previous beliefs so that you can emerge into a new way of life.

I focus this first book in the series with a transmission centered in awareness because to experience and then genuinely embody the power within, one must wholeheartedly believe in and trust that divinity.

By recalling the past, you subconsciously hold onto the patterns, as if the karmic imprint continues to repeat itself in different ways throughout your life. Without cultivating this awareness of how adverse outcomes are manifested, we continue the spiraling cycle of behaviors.

In every moment, you are supported. It is simply a matter of tapping into that support and embodying the present moment. It's not about the moments to come, but the expansion now where you can feel when the divine presence of your spirit.

Your worth is not defined by your material possessions or physical appearance. Those are merely reflections. Knowing your truth and worth does not correlate with monetary value. It pertains to how you interact with the world and the boundaries you set. I mention those limitations because we are only affected by what we allow into our space.

As you ascend, it is increasingly important to constantly re-evaluate what type of energy and situations you are available for. In limiting what you are open to energetically, you can readily welcome more miracles and manifestations.

In this moment, you are creating space for this heart-centered expansion. I am sharing this transmission and bringing healing power to your journey. Allow yourself to keep an open mind to receive the activation through my words.

There comes a divide between those who can understand themselves as multi-dimensional beings and those imprisoned by their own consciousness. Connecting to this source of truth within is the key to unlocking these soul contracts and understanding the ancient codes that you've been embedded with since the beginning of creation. These primordial codes have always existed; the lesson is to awaken your knowledge and remember such codes.

They have chosen me to carry this message for you to remember your divinity. I am bringing into focus the truth that was already inside your life vessel. Here, I will expand the role of human consciousness and teach you how to develop portals of spiritual intelligence.

This will be a healing experience to empower your understanding of the universe. However, for unity to bloom, you must learn how to ascend and utilize consciousness to access your primordial gifts, which have existed since the beginning of creation.

I am teaching you how to naturally expand your intuition's messages. Energy can be physically changed, worked with, held, and released through the breath and other means of meditation and movement that I describe throughout this transmission and other books in this series.

The journey of connection should always start first within, before seeking any external solution. Everything that a plant medicine or psychedelic substance may change for you can also be done without introducing anything from outside of yourself.

As humans, we've been conditioned to want the quick fix, but the most meaningful journey occurs simply by facing yourself. You are learning how to sit with the shadows and transmute them into unstoppable clarity and power.

You can release the weight of emotion and fear, letting it go as you ignite the connection to self. Through this source of truth, you can access depths of yourself beyond what you may have known to be true for your entire life.

There is no shame in being faced with darkness or experiencing hurt in the past, as many of us have faced trauma or perpetuated the cycle of self-damaging behaviors. To know your light requires making peace with your past and transmuting that pain, anger, guilt, and mourning into pure potentiality and love.

Even in the face of violence or poverty, love exists within us, and through the embodiment of that love, we can realize that nothing else matters. No matter your situation or what you have encountered in your physical world, there is the opportunity to know yourself. Beyond self is your connection to source, God, or however you identify with the forces of creation, and within that force is your personal power.

I am simply the conduit illuminating what was already there. Giving it essence and meaning beyond the realities you've learned to perceive. You will experience infinite miracles as you unlock these codes to your ascension.

Many things you've been seeking clarity on will become crystal clear, and the resistance will not disappear, but your perspective of such challenges will change. The deeper you look inside, the more you will understand your motivations for things and the reasoning behind your behavior.

The power that you control is meant to be explored. I am activating the playfulness and joy in your essence, so you can experience true fulfillment without the negative weight of emotion and trauma. Rather than continuously questioning your desires, you will progress forward to a place of surety and wholeness. That comes from being centered in knowingness, allowing you to fully understand and expand your life experience.

Re-igniting this experience of how we teach other generations, our children, and those who come across our path. For you to become more conscious of how our energy influences those around us.

I am the messenger for you to embark on the journey within and to access this information of elevated consciousness and quantum healing available in every moment. I've channeled these words through the ancestors as a conduit of the knowledge we are meant to possess.

Mastering yourself is not allowing others to guide your path, or at least not allowing other human beings to alter the course. It may seem strange to read that if you are new to the concept of divinity, but it is your soulful birthright to receive messages from the God within and your ancestors rather than following the direction created by other forces in this physical reality.

When you ignore those higher messages, warning signs or gut feelings will lead to further stress. You may not need to instantly become averse to a situation if your intuition guides the path elsewhere. Seek to cultivate a deeper awareness of such guidance and how to expand your power.

The awareness exists now, so stay focused on preserving your internal peace rather than being vulnerable to influence or energy vampire situations. Even if it may seem optimistic in the moment, be sure to listen to your inner compass. Where are you being guided?

You don't need assurance or convincing from others when the surety inside exists because you find that knowingness internally. The process of healing is now unfolding for your highest good. And you will continue to access more profound clarity on what is meant for you versus where you need to assert boundaries.

This is the bridge between the current version of yourself and the sacred transformation of source energy. You will leave this experience with a new understanding of yourself and your power. Deeply seated within you already is the knowledge of how to bring this transformation and connection. The activation process occurs through my words as I allow the guides to speak through my words. These are channeled messages of sacred evolution.

I've experienced the full potentiality of darkness and light creation for all facets to be used as a tool for expansion. The intent is to teach you to balance all facets of yourself and access your soul contracts. You will understand the meaning of the magic within and the natural ways for you to work with your energies. This is an opportunity to access your higher self and the infinite potential that you possess.

You receive information from the source of life within you every moment. I refer to this as the voice of your intuition; you feel this transmission as a gut feeling or guidance. However, when the channel is open, the flow of knowledge is constant rather than an occasional burst of information. This deeper messaging always exists, but releasing worry and negative vibrations enables you to fully access the gifts you are meant to receive.

The ultimate goal is to allow yourself to be guided even when the darkness is weighing on your vibration because it is improbable that the world will exist without polarity and the presence of negative energy. "As above, so below" means that everything in the light also exists in the darkness. The point is to focus less on being on a single side of this polarity and step into the embodiment of your totality, which represents all sides and energies you possess.

You will approach the darkness and difficulty you face from a new perspective. Your previously narrow path will be expanded infinitely through your connection to the light and primordial intelligence.

The energies of consciousness and the miracles within are not to be ignored or feared but to be worked with as they bring you a deeper inspection of your own code. Your gift to see into and channel those energies is not to be taken lightly, as it is a constant journey of introspection and growth.

I've been gifted with the power to connect more people to this consciousness. However, it requires a commitment to reading this book series and doing the inner work. Dedication to self-mastery should not waiver based on what may or may not come into your path. If you are too focused on the details ahead, you tend to miss the full expansiveness of the present moment.

When you finish the transmission, allow yourself some dedicated time to implement these lessons in a way that feels good to you and to embody the channel of truth within.

Move through this journey with an open mind because your beliefs are the only limits you will experience. Whether this experience is entirely new to you or you are already on the path of divinity, I am here to activate your spiritual destiny. You will access and understand your power as a gift of ascension and eternal fulfillment.

The limits and separation built into modern society take you away from your internal messaging through the subconscious conditioning we've experienced. Think social media, the news, mass mandates, and other manmade forms of influence such as schooling and regulation.

Our ancestors did not have all the rigid structures and institutions present today; however, they were free to think and create. We've been taught to believe things so far from the truth that it leads to confusion and, ultimately, more questions about why we are here. I am teaching you to connect with your true purpose and transcend beyond what you may have learned or experienced.

We are conditioned to think we must strive toward wealth, whereas material things such as money are all constructed beliefs. In our sovereignty, we are free to experience abundance and all of the miracles life brings. Rather than continuing to experience struggle or hardship, you are opening to receive your birthright to true fulfillment.

Money and things in the physical world are all a product of energy, so accessing your purest state of being is a state of alignment where your contributions compensate you through the impact you make.

Ask yourself: are you living to experience your true potential and share that with others, or are you becoming comfortable with what you have now?

How are you making contributions with your impact rather than focusing your life around the attainment of material things?

The root of comfort or pleasure-seeking behaviors is wanting to avoid pain or discomfort. The actuality of this perspective is that comfort is slowly killing you and your dreams. This is reframing your view that comfort is not always the goal, as it can lead to stagnancy and becoming complacent based on monetary or situational attainment.

Chapter 4
Infinite Creation

Trusting in divine guidance requires realizing that it may feel good, but that comfort does not lead to actual growth. Start viewing your actions through a different lens; recognizing where the patterns lie won't take long. You tap into the true power when you have awareness and choose to put forth and attract the energy of love.

Because when you have a grounding in that power, that potency attracts the right people and situations to you. As you shift into your source of alignment within, your behavior patterns will begin to flow more freely without the restriction or emotion of the mind. Instead of allowing the mind to flood us with emotion, worry, and attachment to physical matter, use the energy from the heart to make connections and feel nature's miracles.

Society has come so far in reconnecting with the holistic ways of our ancestors. This will be a continuous relearning process.

Still, the intelligence that comes from knowing your power is one of humanity's greatest gifts. This is a calling for you to detach from the ego, end pleasure-seeking behavior and use your energy in a way that feels expansive in all moments.

When you understand the potency of your energy, you can harness it to accelerate your soul's mission. Rather than depleting your life force and engaging in closed-minded situations, you are entering a massive transformation where you are untethered to belief, limitation, or emotion.

Many people are seeking too much fulfillment from the outside world and haven't even begun the journey or perspective of going back within. Returning to remember home and the courage that is inside you can be used to bring harmony to the world. Your place in this ascension is to reach your highest perspective of self because that is where freedom exists.

If you've heard the concept of heaven on earth, in essence, this means that the power of God exists within us all. Instead of personifying the forces of creation as an external thing, you are cultivating the awareness within.

Don't think you will wake up tomorrow, and it will all be revealed in one night of spiritual evolution. This is the space for you to access a new perspective. It is a process of connecting to a deeper consciousness, where you can use your intuition to evolve and understand your place in this matrix beneath all illusions.

Allow yourself to expand into this feeling as the trust comes from you. The more you surrender, you will gain more awareness and move with intention rather than being stuck with the repeating question, "Who am I?" You are an infinite creator. You are pure light, coming from the darkness to ascend into the fullness of life.

Tap into the free-flowing expression of you, as you are everything created from the fabric of existence, gifted with this life in human form. You are in the vibration of love as my words bring more light into your soul.

To feel the facets of life beyond your imagination comes the comprehension of alchemy. But before you understand the fundamentals of such transformation, you are cultivating an awareness of your extraordinary nature. Your power goes beyond the forces of creation to the deeper levels of existence and vibration.

The light you have is pure love. You deserve to know and experience all of this light because you are the life force of this universe. When you tap into that force, the result is accessing knowledge and growth.

If we hold onto darkness or depression and the body harbors that dense energy, it can be easily transformed with intention. This new perspective is that of enlightenment rather than lack.

You will step into the ever-changing state of ascension rather than continue to burrow through overwhelming troubles or stress. All those shadows and their weight can be released as you accelerate in the path forward. Feel the courage overflow in your body as you face your fears and whatever has been getting in the way of your highest self.

There has been much to distract you from within and the love that moves through you. Many distractions are rooted so deeply that you must dive into your consciousness to cultivate awareness of what is leading you astray.

While sometimes that awareness is as simple as evaluating the time you spend consuming media, the deeper introspection begins with assessing what influences your decisions. This will be a continuous process of recognizing where you are vulnerable or distracted and choosing to embody love rather than fear or worry.

Define the intentions you have for this journey each and every day, and remain focused on your divine path. I am preparing you to access the depths of your psyche, wherein lies the truth. Your inner knowledge guides the way, where you will understand there is no prescribed way to the future, nor should you attempt to define those details.

The path forward is journeying within and learning to trust the process. In the present moment, you can choose to dwell on the mysteries or perceived difficulties you've been confronted by or move forward and connect to the truth of your desires.

State your intentions to the universe. Speak into existence what you want, and that verbal permission alone will call for it to be brought into creation. Give thanks for your divinity as you begin to walk toward the exploration of your inner world.

Trust that this inner essence is far greater and more fulfilling than you would have ever imagined. As you express gratitude, ground yourself in this reality and your enlightened pathway to the higher vibrational knowingness and truth.

If you believe in suffering, struggle, and hard work, that is the life you will experience. Be careful of the energies you speak of, as the outcome is much more fulfilling when you hold the constant belief that your life is a blissful pathway to divine light and intelligence.

Just as you can use your words to create positive manifestations, this process can work in reverse. This is where you should become more conscious of the words you speak, even when things don't seem to be going your way. Inviting that lack or worry will perpetuate the cycle of struggle.

In every moment, you have the opportunity to transform that fear into love through your energetic frequency and how you speak. Trust the process is working for you, and reframe those unfavorable circumstances through the perspective of love, gratitude, and abundance.

Build on the intention to transform negative memories, traumas, or societal conditioning and ease them into gratitude and thanks, and you will continue to feel the weight lifting. Rather than recall the past and repeat those negative patterns, give yourself permission to release any burdens you've held onto or buried.

Now, as our physical body feels lighter through those intentions, we are putting forth what we no longer seek to hold onto. Releasing the pain, expectations, and hurt held in our physical, mental, spiritual, and etheric bodies. Recognize that it does not belong to you and is not meant for you to bury inside. Over time you've been taught to suppress or cover up those feelings rather than feel their gratitude and then release them.

If something has been challenging, move past those energies and come to an understanding of where your inner compass leads you. By cultivating awareness, we use alchemy principles to manifest beauty, wisdom, and the expansion of love.

The validation of what you want comes from the messaging you receive within. Not from visualization presented from the outside world. When your intuition keeps drawing you back to certain energies, there is guidance to follow and often hard realizations that reveal those patterns you need to release.

Without alchemy, how can we expect to surrender and feel whole if the darkness is one-sided? By one-sided, I mean that negative vibrations and lower dimensions are holding us back into this lower reality, sometimes to the degree where negative influences are taking control.

Alchemy is the process of transferring the darkness from a polar negative to feelings of bliss, enchantment, and, most importantly, expansion. You are the one to perform this process and realize the possibilities of your ascension. The power of transformation lies within your expression of love and gratitude.

With visual representations of the ascension process, we categorize the stages of love and enlightenment, but what if the true power of creation is beyond solid, distinguishable forms? As humans, we want to see where we are in the process, but the true nature of that process can never be quantified or depicted on a stage-by-stage chart.

It is through your own spiritual insights that the spark of creation blossoms. Your ideas come into form, and that catapults new matter, which with the right intention, can impact many people, even beyond what traditional emotion would be considered. Your collective purpose is determined by how you bring value to the unified consciousness, not just your own personal achievements.

When the pathway becomes unclear, call upon your inner essence to bring forth a deeper perspective beneath the layers of confusion. The fog exists when your attention is not in alignment with your actions.

Always remember the importance of words, both written and spoken. If you speak of something, it's driving the forces where your vibrations are moving. The power of such words is comparable to that of creation itself because, through words, you are cultivating the fulfillment of that manifestation.

When you fully realize the vibration of what you are destined for, the universe steps in to bring forth the fruits of divinity. Breathe into that feeling of expansion. What does it feel like to have that joy deep within your soul? To only attract things in your highest good and for those things that are not aligned to fall away with no conflict.

The purpose of life is so far beyond us; when we dive into the depth of our spirit, we then become connected to the infinite nature of life. The guidance within is the place that is the source of true discernment and decision-making, as well as alignment and growth.

The mastery of perception comes from knowingness, and this level of ascension is when you reach the true frequency of love and your highest self. We are given the illusion of choice, but it is not a matter of defining these choices when you are led through spirit.

You may initially feel influenced toward a particular decision, but spirit, source, or however you want to refer to the forces of creation, that higher self has an entirely different set of ideas. Listening to that guidance will continue to bring you into a state of fulfillment and joy.

When unhappiness or complacency sets in, the resistance leads you to question your integrity. These questions flood your mind when you do not trust the path revealed within. Instead of placing the trust factors externally and searching for clarity from external influences or opinions, that introspection goes within, deep into the roots of creation.

As you integrate the lessons from your current and past life experiences, you will jump into a new understanding of what it means to trust yourself. The power within will guide you, so believe that the internal messaging always comes through. Utilizing such forces to bring about expansion is the ultimate mission. Remember your magic.

You will learn to embrace the wholeness of self and prepare to join forces with others with the same collective purpose. This holds true at any level of interaction. Avoid seeking out people unaware of this power or who don't have your best interests at heart. It becomes evident that anyone who has to convince you with their words may not be in complete integrity because your internal source of wisdom knows differently.

You don't have to prove your worthiness; that would be putting the energy of lack inside your body. In that sense, the knowingness you possess answers all. Inside that truth is the purity where you can still learn to have compassion for your shadows.

Seek to understand and appreciate all sides of yourself without projecting shadows or downing others because it is all a mirror reflecting your internal turmoil.

We find the truth of our existence and the keys to our primordial codes through remembrance. If you are unfamiliar with the term primordial, think of your ancient past lives as your body contains the knowledge and intellect of many lifetimes and ancestors before you.

Alchemize all of your sadness and negative emotion into celebration and laughter. This process of alchemy is achieved by facing whatever the negative emotion is and envisioning that emotion being completely released. Trust that it is okay to feel through those perceptions of pain or negativity.

Allow the pain you are holding to rise and be released outside your body. Bring your awareness and intention to the positive energy you wish to welcome in. Not only are you using the power of manifestation to turn the negative into positive, but you are increasing the frequency of your light body.

Don't let attachment or the desire for validation prevent you from coming into the greater whole of who you really are. You are whole in this existence. When your heart is full of gratitude, any door that appears closed can and will open for an even greater miracle to come through.

Love is unconditional, understanding, and courageous. In the place of anger or cutting cords, send compassion for where that person is in this present moment. You cannot fault a person for reflecting a mirror of what you are going through.

Set the boundaries, and they will be respected as you honor yourself and your personal practices, such as self-care or celibacy. It doesn't necessarily mean abstaining from sex or sharing energy permanently but being more conscious of your connections and how you are influenced by what is external.

For a genuine spiritual connection to exist, you have to put in the work. Do not turn away when things get complicated. The light honors you and knows your true potential. You wouldn't have the endurance or experience today if you weren't meant to elevate to this higher level of consciousness.

I am activating the energy by channeling ancestral wisdom and the voice of the divine within you. This power cannot be stopped when you encounter perceived challenges; simply surrender and allow the spirit to speak through you. Trust that these words are here to activate your spiritual power.

Chapter 5
Trusting Spirit to Guide

As the voice of your intuition comes through you, feel the strengthening of your spirit. Celebrate and rejoice in the beauty of this messaging as it all exists in love. The knowledge of that love is now ingrained in your soul. As it activates, you remember who you are.

The messengers of the angels, the gods, the ancestors, and the plants; through you, they birth new beauty into the world through selfless service and the embodiment of divine intelligence.

Envision yourself as a tiny cosmic light in this infinite universe. In knowing true love, you can expand on your purpose and express yourself through all forms of creation.

I give you this gift of understanding to expand further as you continue to read the books in this series and do the work inside. Even though you've been conditioned to fear death or think it will be painful, there are no negative experiences in this realm. Only the perception of such.

You feel yourself now drifting into a vortex for transformation. A portal that transmutes anything that doesn't serve you. Let it all go and surrender in the present moment. Surrender in this moment now.

You will feel the true power when you come out the other side of the surrender. Returning to source energy where your intention is to remember the true bliss. This pure joy of existence from the nothingness where no weight or burden exists. Belief has no barriers because those beliefs were manufactured in the first place.

When you feel the tension coming up in the moment, trust that you are safe to express and release how you feel. Do not hold onto it or allow it to start manifesting from a hostile place. Don't allow people to project their egos or insecurities on you; always retain control over your reality and manifestations.

Part of establishing boundaries is being so transparent with them that your sense of self is always unwavering. Communicate those boundaries without feeling guilty or like you are letting someone down. When those boundaries are let down, don't condemn your decisions but learn from where you allow that vulnerability to turn you away from your true desires.

If your hopes and dreams are unclear at any given moment, at least set the bar for what you are willing to tolerate. By allowing low quality, you are blocking new miracles from coming in and dimming your own light. Instead, love yourself and know you are enough to always receive in abundance. Sometimes all you need to do is remind yourself of that love rather than repeating old patterns of lack.

When you need to question whether something is empowering, chances are that it may not necessarily be "bad," but that situation or person is not in your highest good. It will not magically become the elevation through your free willpower if that is not what's meant to be in the moment. So instead of being upset or frustrated, just allow things to be as they are by sending love and compassion.

If the truth is revealed and you don't like it, attempting to change it is unnecessary. Let it be. Let yourself be in the fullness of your essence rather than wanting things to change. Find the wholeness and power in your presence as it is now.

Focus on the awareness of self, and when the body starts feeling heaviness or sensations that are building up, bring attention to that. Seek to understand the root and the why, not in the sense of attachment, but to ensure you remain free from negative energy. Rather than harboring resentment because you have no control or a situation isn't necessarily aligned, recognize how that feels in your body and let it go. The surrender enables you to step into the alchemy and change what needs to blossom.

Instead of digging further into the physical world to figure out why it's not going your way, ask your intuition, "Why does this upset me? Or "Why am I bothered by this?" The deeper you go into your reactions, the more you will realize that the attachment to those feelings is taking you into energy that doesn't belong to you. That isn't meant for you to hold onto long-term. Feel that sensation, observe the lesson, and release.

Leave that external energy where it is and keep asking yourself questions until you understand the point at which your power is given away. You are forcing yourself to return to that power through self-realization rather than continue down a destructive path of emotion. Knowing your ancient ways is more important than being taken away from your source of grounding in this brief moment.

Seek to continue the depth of your knowingness rather than allowing situational interferences to drive away that remembrance. The path to true freedom exists internally, so next time you sense undesirable feelings, find a place to sit in peace and lead yourself through the revealing questions.

Be in silence and listen to your heart. How do you want the expansion to feel? If you are hurt, don't bottle that pain; just feel what needs to be felt. Tears are a release, just as screaming, movement, writing, and other forms of creative expression are all forms of release. Do what you need to do physically to come face to face with those feelings. In doing that, you are empowered to release that emotion and open yourself to higher ground.

In the magic, you will find love, power, and all that you are meant to be connected with. Think of making life like a ceremony containing all the rituals and actions aligned with your highest good. When something presents itself as outside of that, don't try to control or change it. That is where you start giving your power away and attaching it to emotions such as anger, fear, or frustration.

Instead of asserting control when things don't go your way, lean further into your ability to let go and allow things to be. Then and only then can you wholeheartedly receive without constriction or expectations.

Even if you are genuinely drawn to a situation or someone and know through your divinity that it is aligned, remember that it is all temporary. The assertion of wanting a circumstance to be forever is the act of attaching to worry or anticipation of the future.

Practice shifting the mindset to what is happening now. Even if you want a good thing to last forever, it likely won't. It will be yours in divine timing if it is meant to be. But if life is truly infinite, why waste time trying to attach to something you never had physical control over in the first place?

It's not that you are working towards having that control. When you break it down on such a godly level, it would almost seem silly to attach to anything if you know nothing truly matters. There is no importance beyond what is coming through this present experience. Come to terms with that realization and remind yourself constantly that even if it feels like forever, the reason it is in your life has no meaningful relation to the outcome. You define your reality.

Another example is if your intuition conveys that you are meant to walk with a particular person. Again, this could be true but think deeper into the lesson and the growth in the present rather than worrying about what the future may look like.

It is not your role to force someone to reciprocate the energy or be whatever role in your life that you've been guided towards. Your only responsibility is to be in your integrity and set boundaries to what you are open to in the present moment.

When you cultivate more awareness of what is aligned with your highest good, all will come together. You will crave and continue to recall that knowingness instead of trying to push or pull things one way or the other.

No situation should prevent you from honoring your body, mind, and soul. No matter how that may seem to deliver what you want in life. Don't question your desires; trust them. Questioning would be a force driving you away from your faith and connectedness. The question is whether the thing entering your life is aligned with divine light and not whether it appears like something you desire.

Affirm to yourself, "I am sure of what I want but don't need to rush the timelines," because asserting that type of energy would be straining the greater purpose. Being too concerned with the illusion of such timelines may lead you to less than savory decisions.

When you trust the path and guidance with every fiber of your existence, there is no question of how it comes together. The urgency is that of connecting to your intuition rather than being guided by influence.

Remain open to the flow of infinite miracles you are gifted with every moment. The clearing sometimes must happen in a cascading or intense way so you can be unobstructed and at peace.

Be patient and have gratitude because it is about appreciating the journey to such internal bliss.

There is only room for the expansion of peace and nourishment of your soul. Anything beyond that is centered on egotistic or material desires. When you come from a place of completion and pure potentiality of creation, the only meaningful result is to move forward in your calling. While such a path is also connected with that of the collective, it is yours to continue pushing.

Love is all-knowing and without expectation. Whether we expect something to happen or not, the creation of such expectations leads to disappointment. Instead of expecting from a place of lack, remain fully open and surrender to the lessons in your path. Then comes the point of fully receiving what is meant for you in this experience.

Look for everlasting love in every experience, even those that wouldn't seem optimistic at first glance. To open up to the pure joy of the universe, we have to be able to laugh at and love ourselves. Completion is found through your own divinity.

Instead of seeking that wholeness and validation from encounters or even just seeking some temporary fun, focus on your path. What feels expansive in that process? You are cultivating a sense of peace and serenity that cannot be found through monetary sources, other beings, or external places.

In nature, none of the illusionary conditioning or need to reach a destination of completion matters. Spirit is just free. Whenever you feel overwhelmed, take a moment to look outside and observe how the trees move with the breeze. This serves as a reminder of your ability to be unrestricted while remaining firmly rooted in your source of power.

The nothingness is a place of such pure potentiality and embodiment of power. Claiming this place of divinity does require you to let go of all attachments to satisfaction. This separates source intelligence from the belief that you need to seek out any answers externally.

You are over-abundant in bliss simply by existing in the void of expansion. We revisit these places of fear and resentment to remove the barriers and weight or avoid discomfort. Not only are these feelings limiting, but they bring us out of our true essence. As you continue to access and develop your spiritual gifts, you realize that these dreams will come true with ease. That there really is no such thing as fear.

To cultivate an unshakable effect on your power, you first need to rewire your thought process away from the standard script of the ego: to perform or to go outside of the self. Because when we go within, the understanding changes. The separation fades away as you access the connection to All That Is.

You understand that reality's true nature is not to perform, impress, or experience pleasure. If there is an excessive indulgence in friends, sexual relations, or other material things, the focus on the internal messaging almost immediately diminishes.

How do you expect to create magic if you cannot even feel or see the magic within you? The ascended reality exists when you remain within yourself to expand and feel supported in every moment.

Being focused on the wrong things becomes less important when you know where home is within you. Because no matter what happens in your external world as the tides are shifting, you know how to respond. You already know and trust the flame of truth within. As you learn and access this deeply rooted knowledge, your actions and manifestations reflect that sense of direction rather than the lower vibrational messaging fed from influences in the physical world.

This is the activation where you will begin to see yourself as a vessel of potentiality. Where anything can be created in the light. Instead of holding onto negativity or reverting to old patterns, we exist in the natural feelings of love, joy, and abundance. Life is no longer forced because you are vibrating in alignment with your destiny.

Manifestation is simple when you're tuned into the channel of infinite light. This place exists inside as a source of divinity and miracles. For you to see for yourself and experience those miracles is the greatest gift for me to give.

Everything you've ever wanted is already yours. We have desires because our soul is already connected to that manifestation. The creation of those manifestations extends beyond the feeling or vibration.

It is first the belief and the knowingness, then allowing your body to release tension and to receive. Finally, let go of all that is no longer serving you, that which binds you to a lower realm and allows attachment to negative patterns, people, or things.

At this point, you must be aware of the things that drain your energy. Fear makes us hold onto places, material belongings, or people. Fear of being alone, fear of starting over, or fear of letting go.

The realization is not to fight the fear necessarily but to realize that these beliefs themselves are an illusion, that the fear is manufactured and was never real to begin with. You are feeding these frequencies when you allow yourself to stagnate or fall back to old patterns of behavior. Fear, anxiety, worry, or other low vibrational feelings will pass as you learn to connect to the messaging from your true self.

Challenges or pain are not things to be feared in actuality. Our conditioning leads us to avoid adversity, such as physical discomfort, or when a pursuit has an unknown outcome. You wouldn't be searching for pain, but on the other side of the fear is often something incredible.

The unknown is where the miracles exist. We all have the connection to allow spiritual forces and create a new life experience.

I once entered a transcendental meditation. Before the start of the meditation, I was so overwhelmed with fear that my stomach felt uneasy. I was resistant to feeling something beyond what I believed to be true. Despite this emotional state, I continued deeper into the meditation.

While entering the spiritual realm, the weight of my stomach kept trying to pull me back to the fear-based emotions. Instead of transcending altogether, I was brought to a vision of what fear looked like. In a sense, my physical self was trying to keep me grounded in the chaos that was going on around me.

Fear is not a physical object, nor can the beliefs associated with fear be viewed as "material" or be seen in any aspect of physicality. Instead of seeing what these thoughts looked like, I was taken to a place of darkness. Where I kept myself encapsulated in the portal of fear.

I could see tiny glimmers of light above me but sensed that fear was a place I had constructed. Society conditions us to live in this place of fear, essentially a trap. It's almost like existing in the only place we've known and repeating the same cycles, not knowing anything above that low vibrational frequency. This is our perception.

Bringing forth the embodiment of higher consciousness starts with the way you think, and then it extends to the awareness of self and your intuition.

Chapter 6
Release and Rise

The ascension process is about seeing beyond the limitations that we are taught to believe. To release the fear without being tempted to reattach when the unknown approaches because, in this space, we find quantum expansion. As you perpetually raise your vibration, you discover new heights of peace and love.

These negative thoughts will cease to exist when we realize our true self has no attachment to fear. Instead, emotions like anxiety, sadness, and anger are responses we've learned from our surroundings.

The true state of this existence is having a constant connection to higher guidance rather than being plagued by the weight of such emotional influences. This is a natural perception, the one our ancestors depicted in the cave paintings, which is the original state of humanity.

However, in today's society, much of our divinity has been suppressed since birth. Not that it is necessarily the fault of anyone involved in our upbringing, but the world is so convoluted it has brought us far away from the source of truth inside ourselves. Spiritual awakening aims to strengthen the connection to self, where traumas can be released rather than accumulating more energetic weight.

Learning to return home starts with remembrance. Come back to your true home within. No longer allowing your reality to be dictated by what you've experienced in the past. Because living truly in the moment happens when you let go of low-dimensional patterns holding you back.

It is time to release control and open yourself to experience all that is to be loved and shared. You are meant to be in this greatness, and your actions will be unstoppable; when you truly step into that energy. As you continue through this activation, the work will occur on a quantum level bringing back this remembrance as you come face to face with your shadows.

Amplifying negative feelings can lead to an emotional state that does not significantly contribute to your growth. Darkness cannot drive you out of the darkness. But how can you truly access the light without fully understanding the evil forces? I spent years running from demons only to realize that fear exists from giving up power to those negative forces or emotions. You can know the existence of such darkness without attaching to it.

When people talk about selling their souls, they relinquish their power in exchange for material or external things. It is one thing to understand the dark side of ourselves; it is another to shine our light in the darkness instead of falling into depression or stagnancy from lower vibrational attachments. Opting for the easy way tends to come with energetic consequences in the long run.

From infancy to adulthood, we learn to worry. Often the fear-based mindset is not something you've consciously chosen to adopt. But it is something embedded into our thought processes by the mass media, government, and almost every external influence.

From meeting many individuals traumatized by organized religion or crime, I've witnessed how such strong influences or trauma during your upbringing can embed certain limiting beliefs or ways of life.

Even if you didn't have a terrible upbringing or what you may consider as trauma, conditioning has occurred from points outside of you from birth. The lesson here is that you will continue to face ideals or concepts that did not come from the source of guidance within. Your role is first to have conscious awareness and then be able to transmute such forces or information to a positive result.

We will cover the transmutation process in the later chapters of this book; just know that it is turning darkness and pain into positivity and light.

The key to progress here is to disconnect. Even when you cannot necessarily be in a physical place to do so, finding a moment of peace allows you to think from the inside versus searching outside of yourself. Many advocate for plant medicine to achieve this, but it can still be done using breath alone, where nothing else is required. So while you can achieve higher consciousness by working with such sacred plants, first do the work within yourself before having a psychedelic experience.

I believe in the power of such medicines, but my role is to teach you how to achieve such transformation without substance because every single piece of your healing and expansion exists within you. And you are in the right place, in the Here and Now, where all your dreams are naturally achieved.

I am here to shift the paradigms in your healing journey. To empower the truth and to help you realize where distractions exist. It is easy to find comfort and complacency in places where we should push past with growth instead. Downward spirals tend to happen when we don't seek to push the boundaries of what is possible.

The most powerful space for introspection exists with a clear mind. Where you can welcome abundance with ease and are not surrounded by negative influences. Sometimes numbing ourselves or relying on external substances can be a distraction within itself.

When looking for peace in the outside world, the only thing you find is missing or fragmented pieces. Those pieces will never seem to fit together for the simple fact that you are looking outwards. Find a moment to pause from your current cycles and look at things from a more conscious perspective.

Shifting into the frequency of harmony starts with recognizing the behaviors that are not aligned with the fiber of your true being. It is not so much our surroundings that are toxic but how we enable our energy to connect with others. That is what leads to that harmful interference. In some matters, you may not have an immediate choice to change who you are surrounded by. This is where it becomes imperative to be conscious of where you are creating energetic ties with those individuals or circumstances.

As your healing journey continues and you hold gratitude for the lessons along the way, you will see things exactly as they are. Not what other people or forces of influence want you to see. The only truth that exists is within.

When you remove the veil of confusion, you permit yourself the birthright to openly receive the purpose you are destined for in this lifetime. It is not a fantasy or something you dream of; it is something you set into motion with the energetic parameters already existing within your genetic ancestry and spiritual coding. Those desires would not exist inside if they weren't already meant for you to possess.

As the approach to living in your purest essence is one of trusting that the highest possible outcome will be forthcoming, you feel the fullness of the energy expanding into your soul. The wholeness that always existed will carry you effortlessly into your manifestations. Therefore, hold reverence and gratitude at all times, so you can remain tuned into that inner source of intelligence and divinity.

The past and the future will attempt to invade your consciousness and shift you away from the bliss in the Here and Now. Use the breath to recenter in the present moment rather than attaching to worries, fear, or repeating patterns. Simply focus on the feed of your divine intuition, where you continuously connect and feel that connection to the source of All That Is.

In this space, you will find truth, peace, and simplicity when you no longer allow the past or worries to paralyze you. By doing so, you stop feeding that particular vibration. We can be in the moment simply by practicing non-attachment to such negative feelings. Free, unrestricted, and whole.

Allow your body to move and overcome habits that are weighing you down. Personal development would materialize as setting goals and commitments; however, your actual growth in the moment happens without attaching to the future. You are not worried about the what or how; simply focus on the feeling of love and amplify the emotions associated with your manifestations.

You are entering a new realm where the test of time defies standard logic. Don't let the exhaustion or other physical symptoms of ascension drive a wedge between your goals. Your power accelerates as you seize new heights in this journey.

Just as your body could be feeling down, your perception is playing tricks on you in the sense that you are creating the experience in this moment. So if you believe you are on the cusp of a breakthrough, continue to lean into that expansiveness and feel the weight shifting.

There will be many people and situations to test your boundaries. Time after time. Every time. This is not a reason to let your guard down. On the contrary, this ensures that you will actually enforce your boundaries. The concept of boundaries exists so people or situations cannot invade your personal, spiritual energy. It is okay if others perceive you as cold-hearted because that is their projection, not the energy you put into the situation.

Anything external to you is merely a reflection of sorts. A reflection of you. The question remains, is it a reflection of your traumas that you are closing off access to or failing to recognize?

When we are self-aware, the self leads the way and provides its own level of feedback during interactions regarding what we are attracting. This is the same reason why when we ignore the internal messaging, it may come back as a lesson afterward.

It requires internal trust when you listen to your voice, not what someone else presents in your space. This is an important reason not to mistake the confidence of others for actually knowing themselves.

Anyone can feel comfortable and secure by themselves or around you, but that cannot be misinterpreted for progression in life. And it is common for others to portray false hopes or influence your decisions, but your gut instinct will discern the truth in all moments.

The test asks, "do you want your dreams more than this person?" If that answer is always yes, then the only reasonable conclusion is that anyone and everyone can potentially get in the way of your divinity if you are not careful. Find your personal clarity first to follow divine guidance rather than being unconsciously swayed from your purpose. Not to cut everyone off, but to drop into the fullness of your presence and remain there.

Constant miracles exist simply by receiving love and welcoming more passion into your life. Creation comes from the peacefulness and fullness inside of your heart. You absorb this greatness. The greatness that exists in all moments, even when no one else is there.

Love is our natural vibration that should not be forced but an inevitable truth to allow, receive and be excited to explore.

When you clear your energy, the path is revealed to ignite your inner fire, so your heart and mind can be as one. If you think of the creation process as a celebration, you constantly bring forth new revelations.

As tension arises, continue to release what does not belong to you. Whether by sitting in solitude for a moment or bringing in more elements like oils, candles, feathers, crystals, or anything that carries the vibration of high intelligence. Even without any substance or material tools, your higher connection exists in your heart and every breath you take.

You are shining light into the world and exploring your true capabilities, which are not limited to your physical vessel. Instead of finding complacency or comfort, seek to push forward through the resistance to feel the depths of your ascension process.

Not just to embark on new paths of creation and creative expression but to view life on earth from a different perspective. It is easy to succumb to comfort as a drug. We often fear the uncomfortable, and before long, we notice our present situation feeds into unconscious behaviors that keep us stuck hoping.

Manifesting is not a hope but an unwavering belief in what is already yours.

We establish limits on an infinite reality by accepting things as they first appear. We see ourselves on a lesser level than the capabilities that are naturally present. This will be a continuous process of seeking the deeper meaning behind everything we attract and come into contact with. For there is a lesson within it all that is to be integrated for growth into higher dimensions.

Rather than being limited by the negative perspective imposed upon you, this is the alignment with your godliness. Heaven is not a place you go to when you die; it is a place on earth in the Here and Now. You can access this frequency simply by knowing how to come inside yourself to become the bliss and fullness already there.

Dig to the root of your decisions. Question the reason for your behaviors. When you find yourself in a negative pattern of behavior, instead of feeding into shaming yourself, seek to see where that pattern originated. Creating space to welcome the vibration of love means facing what has brought you out of alignment and where you allowed it to happen.

There may have been many places where you've lost yourself or been unable to face who you are. This is your permission to be exactly as you are now. The flaws are meant to be there for you to experience the full depths of consciousness and ascension. You can access your true self and intuitive power even when hurt or physically injured.

This activation is intended to bring you into the infinite presence you are already connected to as a spark to help you understand your gifts. There is no prescription for greatness, but the clarity and action steps will be found through your internal guidance rather than searching for external completion.

Chapter 7
Your Internal Temple

I'm here to remind you of the magic within. Your remembrance of this inner truth. I am illuminating the path for you to cultivate a deeper connection to your spiritual missions and become fully centered in this divine light.

My hope is for you to keep an open mind at all times, free of expectation and judgment, and walk forward with continuous momentum. The intelligence you possess is far beyond what you've learned to be true. So have faith and give thanks for this constant stream of connection.

The occult means hidden. The traditional dictionary may refer to these supernatural, mystical forces as phenomena, but these "secret" powers were not so hidden at the beginning of time. We see this from looking at cave paintings and ancient structures. If you look back into the history of your ancestors' traditions, it is very likely that the art of creation and such practices that in modern times would be perceived as the occult were a part of their daily life.

The only thing for you to know here is that the knowledge of your spiritual powers has likely not been imprinted upon you. Even as you become aware of this light, so much can be happening around you that distracts you from your divine self.

It is not that magic does not exist; the knowledge, codes, and traditions have been kept from us by elite forces in our modern society. I'm not here to convince you of anything or to dive into debunking theories; moreover, to share how my direct experience with the occult forces has revealed the truth for your personal healing journey.

You are simply tuning in to absorb that information yourself, amplifying the power of your ancestral traditions. So rather than me naming off a wide range of different rituals, I'm encouraging you to set aside the time to tune into your intuition. Sit within your spirit and be guided toward the practices meant for you.

In time, you will feel drawn to certain symbols, objects, crystals, flowers, feathers, and other substances that may be used in the practices you create. For example, I've been guided to clear my energy each morning by lighting palo santo and incorporating that as part of my daily meditations. I felt called to this as a way to protect my energy and keep the field free of any heavy spirits.

Be patient as the pathway will continue to reveal itself, especially when you are crystal clear on your mission. There is no doubt when the intent is focused on serving your higher calling. In the work of the spirit, everything you bring into existence is based on these principles of creation; to share the totality of your soul's essence.

It is not a concern with what others know to be accurate; this is your experience to work within the energy of creation. Alchemize the inherently bad parts that do not belong to you in this existence. You are already full of beauty, love, and compassion. By releasing and surrendering, that negative energy is released into higher vibrational frequencies. The burdens are only painful if you attach to that matter.

Instead of holding onto an emotion that is not meant to be kept, your vessel is a conduit for the forces of magic and creation. To contribute to empowerment, depth of connection, and collective expansion.

Your vessel is a temple for sacred creation and alchemy. To develop an understanding of such, it is vital to honor yourself as the holy temple of All That Is. Stop giving your power away or wanting to make others happy. Your role is to observe how spirit guides you into alignment rather than letting external forces influence your path.

Honor the divine inside of you and always reflect in that honoring process "I am." As you continue through the journey and activation in this book, you will see how words are used as a tool for expansion and healing. Speak into creation with light and love rather than using the tongue as a sword; the reflections in the outside world will match the energy you are projecting.

Alchemy has not been forgotten but is now seen as more of an art form than its fundamental role as a pillar of nature. The obstacles presented in our path to divinity are influenced by the ways of modern society. Such practices were established to insert toxicity in our food, household chemicals, and through other inputs such as mainstream media.

It is never a conspiracy or a theory because these things have been proven and studied. If the forces feeding you such poison and information were doing something in your best interest, there wouldn't be a controversy surrounding their intent.

In returning to your ancient ways, you find beauty in everything. You can observe others going through their process and fighting demons without judgment or trying to change it because the focus is on your own self-empowerment.

The surrender holds power as you hold onto nothing and access All That Is in every moment. The freedom in this experience has no bounds as you are not afraid. The goal is to have no fear, not even the fear of death. Fear doesn't really exist.

Trust the opening to pure spirit form is the portal to the new earth experience. Separation from the old, toxic, conditioned ways is necessary to understand the primordial spaces of intelligence that await. You are being brought back into the clarity of your powerful existence.

This is the time to embody these soul contracts and reconnect to what you are destined to create. The act of creation is a natural part of life, but you need awareness first. The answers are found once you've cultivated the ability to release all that is not serving you. Then it becomes an opening process where you attract new things in alignment with your destiny.

I found my power in the most unsuspecting way through dark traumas starting from childhood, but often it is in the darkest places in our lives that we find peace. I spent years aligning with the true essence of my goddess self to learn how to connect with this guidance and truly heal. Sharing it with you is shining light into your darkness so you can move away from the illusion of separation. We all have things to heal, whether grief, trauma, or pain.

You are a small piece in an interconnected realm of life, where the light of your creation can only shine when you've let go and surrendered to All That Is. Use movement, intention, and speech as medicine and your hands as tools of spirit creation, not destruction or stagnancy.

Your pure essence exists in the vibrations and rising of iridescent rainbow light. Stepping into this perception as a warrior of light will give you the new focus on not wasting this light or allowing distractions to take you away from your mission.

When you open yourself to all dimensions of possibility, there are no limiting beliefs of what could be; it is already because you've permanently been embedded with that desire. The thought alone is enough to bring manifestations into your reality, so your focus should be releasing negative thoughts.

If you notice when you perceive yourself as a channel to receive information rather than a vessel to store feelings, it is much easier to acknowledge and release limiting ideals. Perhaps, one's manufactured fears will impede the most progress when your potential lies at the end of the false belief that you are separate from what you want.

The hope for humanity will rest when we are heard. This is the remembrance of your authentic voice. These powerful messages come through me from the ancestors, for I am a conduit for expansion.

We see the physical reality dimension before us, but it is only one fragment of nature's pure essence. Humanity used alchemy to evolve for thousands, possibly millions of years, long before your existence. We've gone so far from these ancestral evolutionary ways when technology asserted control, but they will not be forgotten. This is where the remembrance is being activated within you.

Technology has encouraged unhealthy habits and ways of thinking and led us to seek validation or completion through external means. Shifting your perspective requires being conscious of where and when your vibration is being compromised. If you can take that hard look in the mirror, those energy leaks are easily alchemized into new creations.

Seeing through the vibration of love in a centered state of being, we greet comfort with more comfort. Without realizing that comfort is the greatest addiction there is. This means that if you remain in the same perspective, you feel stuck because none of that pain or negative energy is being released or used toward the expression of light and creativity.

Viewing that heavy, dense energy as an opportunity for growth rather than a setback brings forth an entirely new set of possibilities.

To end the repeated cycle, you learn to trust in the unknown. Trusting the manifestation is created through the complete embodiment of your true calling. This is the greater awareness of All That Is, where there is always the opportunity for you to access and integrate a greater dimension of energy into your life here on earth.

You are now tasked with self-realization, claiming responsibility for all parts of your awareness. How do you surrender to the openness with distractions present in your path? Asking yourself this question will reveal where your focus may be easily influenced, especially if you are unaware of what is pulling you out of your spiritual essence.

This physical plane is simply an illusion, where you don't see or remember the trustworthy guides present at times. You are never alone. You are never disconnected or apart from the oneness that is.

The beauty and joy meant to be experienced in this lifetime are far more incredible than you've dreamed. In this vessel, you walk the earth in pure love. This is undoubtedly one of the greatest gifts from your ancestors, who made that possible for you to carry out the physical work of the spirit.

Indeed you would have fully known your past lives and realms of infinite possibility if not for the constant charade of information streams.

If we seek remembrance of our true home within, infinite love is present. It has never left. Anything outside of that loving bliss is not meant for you to make attachments to. You were always at home in this body. Where now, you ignite a new sense of presence as my words unlock this code within your natural understanding.

The knowingness is one element of your origination, but beyond knowing is unraveling the layers of the onion and understanding how your gifts have emerged in this current lifetime. Wanting something to occur is not the same as manifesting; often, the instinct is to use words to bring it to life. But, beyond using words as a creation to bring it to reality, you are aligning with the inside workings of your spirit.

Seeking to understand the true meaning behind those thoughts brings us back to the zero point of ultimate love, courage, consciousness, and self-expansion. This occurs when we truly move into the present moment, into the joy that is truly our birthright.

When you have the inclination that you are meant for more or "deserve" better, think back to the trustworthy source of that thought. It is rooted in our intuition, our spirit guides who subtly nudge the way forward.

By trusting ourselves, we cultivate a deeper connection with the calling we've been brought to experience.

Opposing forces are labeled so that we personify them as evil. But many need to see how they were made that way and the shadow work that needs to be harnessed to overcome such negative energy.

When we allow the negative vibrations to manifest in the physical body, it creates disease and emotion. Releasing that energy is a challenge, where you will face the most limiting beliefs and trauma residue. Confront your deepest shadows instead of allowing them to consume your mind, body, and spirit.

Because you have the silence to sit with your being, doing so should not make you regret your past, as the assurance will connect you with others who've walked a similar path.

We've spent lifetimes not being heard for our truth and feeling resistance toward full expression. As a spiritual being that exists in many dimensions, sight is just one form of illusion. Trusting in our soul is a feeling of knowingness, feeling into the heart space toward what we are called to do.

In a place of resistance, there is simplicity to be found. The instant transformation occurs when the level of knowingness expands deeper into our subconscious. When you remember to trust in the divine within.

For those who walked blindly to their own spiritual essence, as I did once, this will be a place for you to begin trusting yourself again. Feel the codes embedded into your soul like waves in the ocean that force the waterfall to rise. You are a crystalline body of access to higher intelligence.

Societal conditions have dulled our senses almost to the point of delusion. It is no longer a matter of waking up; it is one of continuing to choose the path of intuition. This voice only exists for you to know the truth and be protected by it. The evil in the world will continue to accelerate; we just choose not to subscribe to the separation and low vibrational energy.

It's less often that you can locate substantive evidence of the origin of supernatural beings. This is for you to realize that every human can release stored energy through your personal connection channel. To trust within, where there is no need to dispel fact versus fiction.

After seeing what I would call the darkest side of the occult, I learned that it is not necessarily bad. That is simply a perception of duality. It just does not belong to your highest good.

When you form attachments or contracts to these dark forces, you feed negative growth in yourself and others. Take mainstream music, for example, where agreements are made that don't serve those celebrities, yet they are signing their soul away in a sense.

But truth be told, we only attract such attachments to low frequencies when we hold onto past events or unresolved feelings. This is the same reason those dark forces target vulnerable people who are disconnected from the power within.

Our vibrational wavelength is defined by the current, the flow, and what we call the Here and Now. The present moment only exists for you to realize the full height of infinite potential. By that, we hold ourselves back with what could be called a shield. Almost like we are creating an entirely new portal, not for a reason intended for quantum leaps, but for a capsule of stagnancy. The path forward is questioning everything separating you from your destiny.

The only way to end that cycle is to come into the full observational spectrum of what is coming through reality. To harness the awareness. The realization is we can physically see only a tiny aspect of reality. The rest is just sensation and guidance from the direction felt inside of our inherent potentiality.

Ascension is learning how to use your powers for acceleration. It is an awakening of self. To put it in perspective, if you live in a world of lack, you will only achieve negativity, negative balance, barriers to entry, and, purely put, brokenness. There is no wholeness when focusing on what you do not have. Know that your desires belong to you inside of the fullness; it only requires the process of receiving them into your material reality.

When you are abundant spiritually, life transforms instantly to support your desires. To reinforce what you already have constant access to in this world where miracles are always present. Your existence leads to expanding consciousness and transcending confusion or lack of depth.

Being a part of this loving consciousness gives us fresh viability for solutions rather than compounding distractions of society. The world shows us the complexity of keeping the veils active, where the compass of impact is measured through connection versus material substance.

We seek approval from people who fail to see beyond the conditioning of modern society. But the real gain is withdrawing from the situation and looking for the root motivation. We negatively categorize someone or circumstantial "bad intentions" for portraying toxicity or a poor outcome; when, in fact, it is a test of polarity. It reflects what you still need to heal.

When there is polarity, we turn to label the two extremes, but by describing that, we are giving them power over us to compel one side of the spectrum versus another. Seeing that is a form of unified consciousness that gives us a different perspective on the input we receive from others. To look at the totality of the situation without judgment or condemnation.

The fear of death fades away when the truth reveals itself. It is not life coming to an end, but a rebirth, a new beginning. These are cycles of repetition. Patterns of truth, behavior, and belief. But what the human mind is capable of is far beyond the extremes or emotions commonly associated with birth and death, but to what exists beyond the limits of our belief.

Chapter 8
Energetic Attachments

If you are curious about why you attract a particular type of person, examine the energy you put into the universe. For example, coming from a place of peace attracts those who will support simplicity. Regardless of the chaos in your external world, your reaction dictates how the energy is received.

Beyond the physical body is the ethereal body, which emanates vibration. So naturally, we gravitate to those who have a similar vibrational frequency. This is the energetic signature placed in the world and is recognized by others.

The adverse effect of allowing stress, fear, and overwhelm to set in; without releasing that buildup of energy; essentially starts radiating from our physical body into the etheric realm. The caution here is not just the energy you are putting out but how you navigate the challenges and resistance that arise when such energy attracts undesired situations.

Many healers refer to cutting energetic cords, which have validity, but in this realm, the act of violence or cutting ensues more dark energy. It is not a physical aspect of scissors cutting through veins but an even more powerful, ritualist act that injures both parties in the spiritual realm.

While this can be attributed to untrained leaders in the spiritual space and the spread of misinformation to shed light on, the reality is that the source of the cord must be removed before that negative connection can be resolved. You are addressing where that attraction started and what needed to be healed before making those energetic attachments.

If you envision what the anatomy of an energetic cord looks like, you will find it is deeply embedded within the source. By that, I mean it comes from the energetic root of yourself and the other person, thing, or place you are energetically connected to.

If your intuition is led to release an attachment, ensure you aren't making a decision prematurely. The act of cutting cords interferes with the exchanging of energies between you and that person or thing. This is where it is vital to reflect on where the attachment came from before taking any dramatic action, whether physically or in your spiritual essence.

Etheric cords are created to respond to emotion or trauma, but the emotional body is often separate from the conscious mind. This means the need for this external emotional connection was created by your genuine need; otherwise, any aspect of your body would not have formed such a cord or attachment. Whether wanted or unwanted, your bonding with this person is almost like a child's comfort blanket. It reflects the emotional representation of an unloved or otherwise hidden aspect of yourself.

We are led towards unfavorable reflections externally when we fail to recognize that truth about ourselves. So again, when you think about the type of energy attached to your emotional body, think of how aggressively ripping away that comforting blanket would feel to the child. Whether that attachment is enjoyable or it is, in fact, displeasing is irrelevant because the act of separation introduces an entirely new trauma.

This person has likely felt toxic or unsafe, making it an unhealthy form of attachment. But it is still an attachment, regardless of being healthy or not. So to examine this bond is more revealing to learn about yourself and what needs to be nourished rather than cutting or blocking it out through an emotionally charged action.

It was not empowering for me to cut energetic cords with my past. In fact, through the healing journey, I learned that the most self-empowering thing I could do was self-reflecting on the emotional injury that I was carrying and how that side of me needed to be nourished.

You can disconnect from one person just to attract a similar cycle with someone else. The introspection examines what led to that attraction or behavior, so you can release that energy rather than repeating another form of the past.

Your clarity exists in the benevolence as you validate these teachings through practice. If I taught ritual, it could be viewed as religious. This process of how you apply these transmissions is much deeper than a label or awareness of what divinity is.

As truth seekers, we see through perceptions based on nothing other than societal programming. In the absence of external influence, what are the decisions we make?

Bringing a specific naming convention to the power beyond traditional thought would be wrong. This is not about religion or modern institutions. Which is only a distraction away from you, trusting that higher guidance inside. Merely reading these words will activate the encoding of your vessel with that remembrance of your truth.

Come into these teachings with an open mind; all I ask from you is to embody your powerful presence. It requires a commitment to growth, not to be limited by belief but to reach the root origin of your divine intelligence.

To know and love yourself for every aspect, even beyond the duality, is a multifaceted evolution of life. And within this lifetime are the lessons of healing and resurgence of ancestral ways. Just as the word respect requires you to hold such reverence for those who've come before you, you are activating that higher power within you.

If your vibration prevents the energy from rising, it will build up and create an excess. Living in complete joy means embodying the present moment without being concerned with what does not belong to you.

Trusting your power is yours alone, not allowing external interference, as it is not your responsibility to change others or their vibration. Your existence relies on trusting the spirit within you. While more energies attach and form bonds or cords, the truth is those that would be observed as excess are often a lesson created to support your transformation.

You are entering a space where vulnerability is your power. Be open to feeling and releasing the weight of what has been holding you back. To feel life's lightness and true beauty, you must first face what energy is stored in the body.

Unlocking your energy field and releasing the negative weight does not mean immediately lifting all burdens. Such a dramatic change would be shocking to your system.

I will guide you through gently tapping into your intuitive gifts and the source of power. Just as the accumulation of junk happens over time, the physical body and mind bury all of the memories and traumas you've experienced. The conscious mind knows its challenges, while the body tends to hold onto the more dense energy layers.

Making changes on all levels of your existence requires consistently shifting your perspective. For you to look deeper into where these memories are stored. As you put these teachings into practice, you'll experience this process and learn to have compassion for the darkness you've experienced. This compassion will evolve your consciousness to an entirely new level.

You can look forward to becoming more aware of what you consume on all levels, from what you see in the media to what goes into your physical body. It is not my role to teach you what to do or what exact path to take; my purpose is to activate the power within you so you can make those aligned changes for yourself.

What no longer serves you goes much deeper than awareness. You will cultivate a sensation of connection to the universe and the joy, intelligence, and expansion that are naturally part of your spiritual essence.

There is a flame that burns internally that can never be blown out or silenced. That is unless you are either not conscious of it or allow external stimuli, such as other people, to influence how you bring that light into the world. The connection to such force must be unshakable for the motivation to increase.

True power inside yourself does not exist over those people in your surroundings; it is underneath the layers of your own soul. So, while the perception may be that internal fire is a destructive force, it can be appropriately used as a source of warmth, positive energy, and nourishment. To be a light on the path illuminating your direction.

These facts and lessons of life present themselves as seemingly unconnected events. But at any level of spiritual awakening, the awareness of interconnectivity brings about a better understanding of where all events fit in, particularly those we'd see as less desirable.

We begin to see life for All That Is as the truth reveals that our human body exists within a multi-dimensional realm; our sensations are created by the energies we emit.

While we exist in the darkness and nothingness, that is where the light of creation brings new miracles into reality.

By embracing the infinite nature of your light, you can easily find comfort even at the darkest stages of life. There is something truly magical about being in tune with the spiritual self because you know that this body is just a vessel for your multi-dimensional soul.

The fact that we are all energy should be viewed from the perspective that this energy creates a wavelength of sound or vibration, both seen and unseen. You can use this power of creation to pull yourself out of negative patterns.

When we are holding onto toxic, damaging, or heavy energy, the result in the body typically leads to further depression and patterns of self-destructive behavior.

Recognizing those triggers and emotions as they are felt enables us to probe into the darkness first and then to rise in our power. You are not meant to ignore the pain or seek numbing mechanisms like substance abuse. Instead, look beneath the surface to places where you can cultivate a deeper awareness and release what is not serving your highest self.

The growth comes from allowing the recognition of the darkness to understand parts of yourself that have yet to be healed. Often the most profound transformations will come from visualizing your shadow self and becoming conscious of your totality, not just the desirable facets.

Have faith that you can reveal all sides of yourself without shame or fear around releasing what would be perceived as unfavorable. However, bringing your true self to the surface isn't all light and abundance.

Before we even get too deep into the darkness, I want to touch on protecting yourself from spiritual influence. With these boundaries in place, we are positioned to expand much more rapidly.

Rather than being tormented by our past and the repercussions of behavior patterns, we implement processes in place to be delivered away from anything not for our highest good. Every single time. It is a no if it doesn't align.

The more you create a secure environment for your situation, the more you activate your power and cast your authority over it. It is one thing to claim that power and another to be shielded from anything that would take away your personal sovereignty.

You will not be shielded from the attacks attempting to come, but you devise your plan of action to remain protected against spiritual warfare that can be the most subtle of attacks seeping into your life and every moment of the day. To stay consciously present, you can take steps to protect yourself.

Protection Practices:

Burn something. I practice this and do it seriously every day to keep my spirit clear, but it is to burn sage or Palo Santo. Feel free to do so if you feel called to some other substance to burn, but those are the most powerful when it comes to clearing.

Stay connected. Find ways to feed your spirit through community because connecting with others who align with the same intentions is essential. If you want to elevate, you cannot isolate yourself. It is not about chasing 1000 people, but a few advancing people can make a difference, even through a virtual connection.

Prioritize self-care. When you know yourself, you will be better prepared to keep your perfect peace. This means staying focused and maintaining a clear mind rather than making negative energy a place for bitterness to grow. That energy has no position in your life.

These simple reminders get you in the mindset of structure and protection against attacks on the spirit. My next book in this series goes much deeper into practices of cultivating your spiritual connection.

Now decoding the mystery of what you've been holding onto is a message from the spirit calling for acknowledgment and deeper healing. We are conditioned to suppress our emotions. But as we go through these changing times, facing the darkness allows you to integrate all parts of yourself into the higher dimensions. Where there is union and freedom.

You are taking the time to sit with your intuition in times of difficulty to know how your energy attracted those adverse circumstances. This is a moment of honesty that you find in meditation or other moments of silence where the aim is to ascertain what behaviors or thoughts are still holding you back. Of course, it takes acknowledgment first, but you also release the attachments to your struggles.

Rather than beating yourself up over circumstances that may or may not have been in your control, hold more gratitude for where those challenges have brought you. In every piece of darkness, there is a lesson in the light.

When you focus on expanding your gratitude, you will be pulled into a higher consciousness in those moments of darkness. This renewed perspective will enable even the rock bottom moments to be transmuted into a horizon of opportunity.

The more you cultivate this awareness, the less emotionally volatile you will feel. Clearing the energy centers from attaching to lower densities can be accomplished through many physical practices.

I recommend exploring Qigong, ecstatic dance, and various forms of energy healing. However, my advice is to make your personal commitments based on the movements you are called to do.

Start by welcoming more consistency with your chosen practices; the results will be astounding. You are cultivating more control and awareness of the energies inside, which makes it much easier to recognize the input from the negative side of yourself. Moving your body and incorporating natural healing practices will feel empowering.

When life is at a crossroads of decision, this process is beyond the knowledge of energetic principles. Nevertheless, it is easy to trust the direction of our intuition simply by tuning into the messaging. In the face of confusion, we silence the internal chatter to see human life for what it truly is.

There is no difference between light and darkness; they are the same thing in the realm of creation, just varying degrees of the same manifestation. To understand the principle further, think about hot and cold temperatures. Upon first impression, you would assume that they are opposite aspects. But if the only difference is in the degrees of temperature, which is a vibration at the most fundamental level, they are simply variations of the same form of matter.

If we apply this to the truth and vibrations of the mind, thinking about the polarity between love and hate, we visualize that these feelings are simply poles of the same form. It then becomes a matter of will to transmute the hatred into the vibration of love within your mind and the mind of others.

This level of mental alchemy applies to all levels of existence, not to radically eliminate the darkness but use willpower to alchemize the state of mind. In doing so, you are devoted to the ascension of healing yourself and the collective whole.

Harboring evil forces or energy should not be shamed but used in the alchemy process toward love and truth. Not allowing ourselves to attach to lower vibrations or spirits that don't serve our highest good but using these forces for divine creation.

Knowing the dark side is better than avoiding that side of the world or yourself. Failing to acknowledge that darkness and totality within us all ultimately gives your power away. The point is to use intention to transform that negativity into the greater good.

The cord between you and that external thing is a gift of knowledge that reveals the source of your insecurities and lessons.

Therefore, a true healer uses the power of that connection to un-cover the truth about one's self. The collective impact becomes where those raising their consciousness elevate and heal those around them.

When life presents challenges, we run to a source of comfort, not realizing that the source of comfort is sitting closer than we think. By seeking external conditions, the attention is drawn to the mindset of seeking, searching, and wandering for some level of completeness.

Remember that godliness existed in you already; the influence may have led you astray. Ignorance leads us to self-sabotaging behaviors, addictions, and poor choices, but the low vibrational forces fade naturally when we seek an understanding of our total-ity. This is not to say they will never approach you again, but the responses will now come from a place of wholeness.

We know our power but fail to face the shadows; we are brought into a hole of disparity and avoidance. The concept of ascension is illuminating your soul and learning how to trans-mute negative energy.

Protection from spirits is not needed from a ritualistic per-spective when deeply grounded in your truth. But we touched on the critical practices of routine spiritual cleansing and self-care because you're not immune to incoming threats.

The knowingness is your connection to the divine and all aspects of your spirit. Which means there is no sense in denying the shadow. Reflecting on your deepest, darkest parts will bring the most growth.

Rather than just acknowledging the worst in ourselves, we have the opportunity to forgive and release any negative tension held around the duality of self. Then, coming into our highest self, we realize that none of that duality or attachment mattered in the first place.

Chapter 9
Finding Alignment

It is only when you shine the light of creation that life begins manifesting as experiences. To change our experiences, the only sensible action is to use energy or effort toward that creation. Describing how the heavens and earth were created would be to depict the same process of how the light you radiate brings forth new miracles.

Life is an infinite miracle, many don't see this as magic, but the simple act of making a goal and calling it into existence works with such principles of natural manifestation.

I'm sharing this transmission to teach you how to ascend through levels of belief that keep you stuck in the dimension of suffering and fear. Those low vibrational feelings attach to our bodies unconsciously. The solution is not to cut off the source of those feelings because we risk losing the knowledge from examining such lessons.

Acceleration starts with recognizing the underlying principles of what we attract and using that to our advantage instead of allowing it to become a nuisance or worry. The reference to repeated patterns of cyclical behavior halt when your awareness level transcends to access the messages from your intuition.

When we examine our motivations, we realize certain things can be avoided simply by tuning inwards instead of seeking solutions elsewhere. In the existence of challenges, there are always several solutions where the universe brings forth alignment.

You only go against the grain in response to insecurity or emotion. That dimension of our bodies can suspend time, meaning that our true-life force is diminished when we attach to such limiting emotions. To shine the light on the impending stress is learning to practice power shielding, where you observe and release the feelings rather than attaching to those inputs.

When the time or the perception of time is expanded, the understanding becomes one of a multitude of realities and timelines existing simultaneously. This is where you understand the illusions and manufactured creation of such time, lending to an entirely new set of possibilities.

You can coexist with those emotions without allowing them to penetrate your energetic field. If you ponder it, your physical body is almost one of the last forms of dimension affected when negative energy enters your path. Yet it is one of the most significant impacts on the rest of our being because that physical matter requires more power than spirit alone.

No matter what someone else does, it can't take you out of the space of love. So open your heart and listen to the medicine of the ceremony of life, moments in meditation, and the constant guidance from your soul. Avoid placing excess importance on things in the external world that have no actual impact on spiritual growth.

The essence of your being is the space created not only in the physical realm but to the depth and the expansive, infinite nature of life on earth. We search for meaning when the truth is revealed in a single-dimensional place, in the present moment.

Bliss is referred to as nothingness because All That Is exists within this space. It is where you realize that at the climax of true enlightenment is your interconnectedness within that infinite place of potentiality.

To bring forth multi-dimensional light, viewing visual perspective beyond the constraints of form is most impactful. Activating those symbols as evidence of the ancestral roots, of their practices, to our previously unknown origins.

I bring you these lessons for you to work with as a gift for alignment, for a resurgence of the spiritual state of being.

In this activation, you rise like a phoenix from the ashes of your perceived past struggles. The smoke will rise, and the fire inside will brighten, just like you ascend into higher states of consciousness.

Keep a candle burning while in meditation and feel the fire illuminate the magic. The purpose of fire without heat would be like the cold with no ice. To explain this: having the natural elements present is essential, expressing gratitude for the various forms of matter.

We introduce the elements of air, fire, water, and earth to change or otherwise transmute creation. These are the building blocks of existence. To connect with our essence, the remembrance of self exists not in the courage we portray but in the truth we hold sacred in ourselves.

The reason for imbalance, depression, and frustration is ignoring that connection to your deeper purpose. Feeling the universe's flow but failing to circulate the energy of wholeness and love.

You will learn how to release the attachment to manufactured perceptions and enter the spirit realm with an understanding of self. With a surety in power that is coded into your vessel.

You've learned only to unlearn and remember. Cut through the layers of self we've constructed as a mechanism to protect ourselves from discomfort.

Tune out the noise. We are not silencing the noise for you to hear your inner voice. You will hear in the presence of chaos and danger; you'll listen to the voice of your intuition leading to the realization of truth. Not the watered-down version we've accepted or fallen for.

The true nature of our existence exists in so many facets; there would be no portal if you don't believe. The portals of advancement are created when the energy is harnessed. It feels good to channel the energy through your body physically, such as with an orgasm, but if that connection is not coming from a sacred bond, your body will need a place to expel that energy.

Indeed, the origin of celibacy comes from celebrating the body as a temple, as a vessel of light. Why allow entry or otherwise enter a temple you are unprepared to face? If you knew the outcome of such energy before making decisions based on desires of the flesh, you would likely choose another route.

This is not a message to say, "think carefully about your partner." Instead, this is a spiritual warning of how such contact can bring the attachment of energetic cords. Separating desires of physicality from trustworthy guidance will lead you to genuinely supportive partners. There is no need for permanency, so take your time when planning too deep into the future.

Indulging in true satisfaction is relinquishing the need to feel complete. Surrendering to the essence of all that is. Because you have no control over what is not and no concern for anything outside of the here and now.

Many different cultures state that seeking pleasure is the root of all evil. If we are seeking to feel good or comfortable, that is where the actual pain exists. Stagnancy occurs when you use temporary things to numb or feel pleasure. Where, in fact, that comfort is sickening.

Sometimes the biggest addictions are the behaviors we refuse to see. Or maybe you're well aware of those addictions and haven't stopped the cycles of trauma response that keep repeating through the risky or otherwise self-inflicted "ill will."

You impose the darkness and sorrow on yourself when you remain in a state of comfort. Such an act of seeking comfort causes problems, where you have the conscious choice to strive for better.

It is not so much a fight or difficulty to get where you want to be or move forward. Perception and belief are what make it hard. Without such expectations or size constraints, things start moving quickly when you let go.

The surrender is where the beauty and bliss come from because you're just allowing things to be and enjoying the present miracles. There's no reason for it to be complicated. Simply open yourself to receive greatness.

Remember, these are the patterns in your subconscious; waking up to them is realizing the power to change. You've only ever been your worst enemy, and now you are entirely centered within. Trust that you only get to know your passion more. And doing so, you learn aspects of yourself better to move forward rooted in your power.

Suppose you notice yourself falling short of your goals or hopes and dreams. There may be something you're avoiding that needs to be faced. Some cycles of behavior or situations may feel attractive, but when you do some reflection, they don't serve your highest good.

Coming face-to-face with deeply rooted traumas and patterns is the way to transcendence. In facing that hardship, you realize that you were only just replaying the thoughts or beliefs from your past or worries about the future.

Being in the moment is where you can let go and release. If you want freedom, always stay in gratitude. When you lay it all down and no longer attach to fear, nothing is left but the beauty and excitement of creation. You lose that fear when you embody that you are already whole.

Such blissfulness should not be hidden with burdens or barriers we've created inside ourselves. True nature is limitless, but we must face what is weighing us down.

The shadow work and integration of knowing our negative facets give us the power to rewrite our story. You hold the Power to change. How can you change something if you fail to acknowledge it?

Speaking from my heart, I've faced some of the deepest traumas in the journey to my divinity. But, the expansion happens when letting it all go. Not attaching to the past anymore. Surrender to everything that is and release anything not meant for your highest good.

It starts with a willingness to be aware of those patterns that are not serving us and to end them. Then, it will be reciprocated if it is meant for you. Otherwise, if a situation seems misleading or someone tries to convince you, it is likely not in divine alignment. Otherwise, everything connected to your destiny will be intuitively led.

The magic exists not only in your interpretation of physical manifestation but your solidity and the resilience of your internal peace. In the knowingness that you possess, the knowingness within that gives you clarity, speed, and direction.

If not done with the proper intent, rituals can invoke sure energetic drainage you are not prepared for. Remember that everything we do in our daily routine can be considered a practice for internal peace.

The energy behind the action and the intention matter because the power of such action or ritual will define whether you are attracting positive or negative energy in your space.

I believe in teaching the energetic principles behind such forces of creation, so let's cover the foundations behind bringing energy into physical form. First, understanding these concepts is important because if your belief and awareness are lacking, such truth will not exist when the forces of manifestation are put forth. Before using these forces for positive change, you must believe in yourself and your natural birthright to power.

There is no one to teach you this other than the elements of nature and internal guidance that you are led to as a product of your embedded desires. Of course, giving you such instructions may be helpful, but the playbook should come from the path revealed inside.

Knowing the power is one facet of the journey, but seeing and experiencing such is the substance of matter changing and manifestations coming to fruition. We become accustomed to how we see the physical aspect of our current reality, but the channel only lends to intelligence beyond what we've been told or can see with our eyes.

This is the same reason why traveling or even astral traveling unlocks certain parts of your DNA. It embeds new codes from nature into the remembrance of true purpose and expansion.

To experience these downloads, you read these words to activate the god within. Your power is discovered deep within these transmissions and the gifts they bring to your life. Reading these words is the initiation, not to be feared, but to be embraced as a gift of intelligence as it reveals itself to you along the journey.

To describe this process would look different if I were to explain it, but I want you to see and feel this for yourself. The journey has prepared you and brought this channel of truth and clarity into your existence. In the Here and Now, you are reminded of your worthiness, light, and pure, potent potentiality.

This sacred initiation is dedicated to the growth of your essence, understanding that essence, and working with it intentionally. The ease comes from leaning into resistance, not to fight the forces of evil but to learn how to transmute that energy into light. Too long spent fighting or holding the perception of struggle rather than transcending brings forth a deeper manifesting of that lower vibration.

This is where you get to know your totality and the truth that we all seek to find. That truth that already exists and has permanently been embedded in this "finding" is merely a rediscovery. Remember who you are.

This is a portal for healing. Instead of repeating the cycle of your pain or negativity, you are tuning into the lessons meant to be received in each moment. Evolution and sustainable growth in your path forward happen by strengthening your internal trust. Not to speed up the achievement of purpose or goals but to surpass the heights of your consciousness. To rise above the beliefs and limitations constructed by the mind.

It is one thing to believe in magic or try to personify divine forces. But the remembrance of self releases the need to attach an ego-centered label to the natural power within.

The solution to fear is smiling in the face of adversity. Simply smiling when the fear starts to take over is enough to realize that the fear is indeed an illusion. The fear does not exist.

In the presence of challenge or heat, we find solidity. There is no true comfort in other people or outside of yourself. Accepting or seeking that comfort to any degree of excess creates an external condition for a source that is not supportive of spiritual growth. What leads to transformation is the ability to let go and trust your internal guides.

Your human body already exists within the vibration of harmony and love. Becoming more conscious of what enters your body, whether it's food, beverage, or who you physically touch, will help you see where that vibration is influenced.

Start each morning with firm intentions, and you will not feel trapped in cycles of stagnancy. You've trusted spirit to bring you this far in the evolution of your gifts, and to embody those gifts is truly special. It's possible you didn't feel that until the transmissions contained in this book, but your contributions matter. You matter.

There will be many things in your path that try to lead you astray. Those distractions become more potent through the ascension progress, further testing your strength, listening, and boundaries.

Chapter 10
Discover Peace

Living in the highest self doesn't mean it's all love and positive vibrations. While, at the core, you are pure love, it is still necessary to examine the root of your tendencies to reveal where vulnerabilities exist.

At every peak in your healing journey, it may feel like you are invincible, and nothing can bring you down. However, the truth is that the higher you elevate, the more that outside forces will try to keep you stuck or brought down to the lower vibration. This is where you go back to solidity to know that you are the source of power, and everything is simply a test of the level of trust within.

By realizing that everything in this physical reality is an illusion of sorts, it becomes much easier to return to the messaging within. To remember the place of nothingness where there is no worry or concern because everyone and everything exists in pure love. Feelings are just visiting for you to be aware of the lesson, then to release.

When we are brought away from that love within can be where things start to get confusing. Brain fog only creeps up when we start holding onto emotions. We were never meant to bury those thoughts. We just feel and release. If something is triggering you, that lesson is yours to uncover. For you to cultivate the understanding so that nothing can take away your peace.

Why get lost in a made-up perspective that is undermining your full potential? The most straightforward part of being is simply to be in your presence. The complications and fear are unnecessary because the truth is encoded within you and your connection to divinity.

Rather than seeking to personify or categorize what religion you resonate with in terms of belief, find that connection within you first to know that you are the light of source, god, or creation; however you want to describe it. Discovering that messaging inside leads to bountiful possibilities and the chance to know how bright the light inside you really is.

Transfiguration is the intent of reaching crystalline clarity in how to use your gifts in the physical world. The clarity never left; it is simply a matter of accessing this higher level of the truth.

Advancement of the self, of the collective toward an impactful purpose, is not a truth of hidden nature but an abundance of aligned action and integration of the guidance. For it is not in the pursuit of a destination but in the beauty and simplicity of life itself. To enjoy and appreciate the lessons along the way.

Surrendering to the emergence of the wild, reconnecting to the spirits of the divine as you ascend. We give this as an offering to the collective consciousness for you to carry out your mission, believing in the forces that bring surety in the face of doubt. False beings present themselves as positive or uplifting, but your intuition tells a different story. Continue trusting that inner guidance.

Use this activation to expand your knowledge, the depth of this experience, and the meaning behind it all. The characters are cast from other lifetimes to support you as you enter this realm. I've activated your remembrance, and now this voice will continue to feed through the messaging within.

The kingdom of creation is within your soul; I am here to activate what you've known beyond a constructed reality. This physical realm is one interpretation to see with the eye. The mind's eye sees differently, not based on material form or a "familiar" concrete sense. Look beyond this known reality to feel the ancestral codes illuminating your soul.

Beneath the shadows lies the nothingness from which all creation is formed. By using our breath to activate specific brain sequences, we command the regeneration of our cells, not just in activating the pineal gland, but of the connections to our power and significance.

Inside of you, the divine connection creates a portal for such out-of-body experiences, one that you don't need to alter yourself to achieve.

In silence and meditation, you have access to everything. This is where the lesson is found because life becomes blissful when you can listen to the constant flow of information. The simplicity of being able to tune out all of the excess noise as you receive divine intelligence.

Those beings who you see operating at a low frequency for their entire life are the ones who hold the heaviest densities of emotion. The weight of your stressors and worries can be alleviated simply by remaining in the present moment of divinity. Through your personal power, there is transcendence and decolonization.

The peace you crave exists in the foundational state of your essence, waiting to be activated. My words ignite your sense of self to heal, manifest, and ascend, but more importantly, to work through the shadows and embody all parts of you.

There are no false ideals or external beings that need to be worshipped. The ascended master inside has experienced past lives that are tremendously different from this current earth's reality.

You are coming into the remembrance of your limitless capabilities and rising above the engineering that conditions us to forget. This is a time to release the storage of past traumas and connect to the source of power that is deeply rooted in your soul.

Shift the perception of mood as energetic matter that takes on body, form, and dimension within unseen wavelengths. This gives you control over what energies you are emitting, to think about it from the scientific and spiritual standpoints of knowing how intention can easily manipulate those wavelengths.

The eminent reality responds even more to spoken word as it emits sound frequency in addition to the densities of emotion emitted. Those worlds translate into an energetic currency where you are sure of yourself and make quantum leaps toward infinite possibilities. Here lies the difference between belief and knowingness because it is in the knowingness that we can be truly guided by the source.

Through learning the ways of our ancestors and seeing from the lens of traditions, rituals, and ceremonies, life moves with so much more intention, purpose, and flow. All four elements of water, air, earth, and fire should continue to be nourished and honored in your practices.

I am initiating access to a channel that extends beyond the messaging in this book. The messaging stems from a voice, our internal voice, many voices beyond us.

As you continue to channel, it becomes more accessible, the voice becomes more robust, and a non-stop flow of inspiration. It will feed through as a constant source, available on demand without ritual or substance.

It continues to be a calming energy you produce; that energy is formed through a focus to yield true enchantment and divinity. Awakening of those who were no longer there. The ancestors never died in the material or traditional sense, but you brought life where it didn't exist in spirit form.

To live and to die is nothing more than to release the attachment to, just as the concept of ego death is a total surrender before the rebirth in spiritual form. We are rebirthing the essence of our true self stripped down to nothingness. The nothingness that contains the power of creation.

Without material substance, we connect to a new source of matter that exists beyond the conventional limitations. For example, if you take a piece of paper and fold it in half, you have two pages, but to do such in an energetic realm would produce a different outcome. Energy is far beyond physical matter.

When the weight of manufactured beliefs and fear is lifted, the lightness will enable us to have a sense of quickness, not in speed but in purity, where the vibration of love is the constant source of miracles.

When we rely on external substances to perform miracles, we can miss the gift of light within ourselves. This is to embody the lessons you receive as an initiation, an opening of sorts. To open new portals where they lie dormant. Creating through focused intention rather than depleting the spirit within.

Pushing through what we otherwise would have allowed in our hearts. To be truly open is a gift of the journey. Not to rationalize what we've experienced but to remain open and continue receiving these messages. The voice of your intuition does not stop, like the flow of a spring that cannot be switched off.

I am using these words to activate your knowledge of self, your remembrance of self so that you can do as you are called.

To be led to the true nature of this journey, you are learning how to trust in these gifts and use this power as a revolution for the future.

You've been through this sacred journey as a gift to be received by the universe with the intent of receiving clarity. We are not here to show you how or where to focus your experience, simply to reveal where you focus too much attention outwardly on everyone else's experiences. Follow the energy of my words, and don't allow physical experiences to deter your focus.

These people around you have been brought to your path for a reason. Death is easy. Comfort is easy. Easy to fold, easy to lay your head down or fight to stay away from the truth. But facing the shadows is your power and the voice to embody your divinity. To shine light where you've previously held onto pain or struggle.

This voice has always existed in your eyes; you see one fragment of the true reality; instead, I've explained exactly what you need to see to have no expectations, no prerequisites for the future. Worry is not a place where you reside in the present.

You've likely felt resistance when accessing the true depths of your heart. So instead of shielding yourself or running when it starts feeling overwhelming, embrace those feelings as a teacher of expansion. For you are the medicine, the space that opens for this expansion.

The lessons are generally missed if you constantly seek "something" or want granular clarity about the destination. It is about learning in every present moment of the journey. To fully embrace that growth and evolution and bring your magic to the universe, trust that the direction is already there. The inside is what creates the outside, certainly not the other way around.

What we are taught to ignore or suppress can also be what brings us the most transformation. This speaks to the things we consume, as the cleaner your vessel, the easier it will be to release what needs to be removed. What never belonged to you in the first place.

Physical ailments such as fatigue, infection, and upset stomach exist on the physical level but stem from a root cause in the spiritual realm. The harmful energy simply reflects what the body needs to heal; sometimes, that may be generations of trauma.

Becoming conscious of deeper-rooted trauma itself may seem like a tricky topic at first glance. When there are many layers of suppressed emotion, one may be unaware of all the experiences that caused this build-up. Revealing every facet of why the trauma exists is unnecessary, but you remember how to release what is stored in the physical body. Do not allow it to build up and get in the way of taking action toward your goals.

The key here is to realize that you don't have to return to that dark place to feel open and no longer hold onto that weight. As humans hold on to loads and loads of baggage or worries, none of that actually belongs inside your vessel.

When you feel yourself taking on negative emotions, allow those feelings to flow through you. In the same way they entered, you will release the emotions that don't belong or otherwise transmute them into power. This same practice is there when you sense that the feelings or energy of others you are surrounded by are starting to wear off on you.

It helps to go outside and place your hands on the earth. Then, as you release that energy through the dirt back to mother earth, imagine yourself sending that energy through the roots of the underground as it is absorbed.

You gave up the comfort to step towards what you truly want. World peace, acceptance, awakening, not just success, money, and luxury but a true impact and connection to this spiritual realm.

Knowing your role as you ascend the confusion and access your true self. There is nothing to search for beyond yourself. Nothing to want beyond what your ancestors wanted for you.

You are the medicine. You are meant to heal yourself, which trickles down to those around you. The quest is not about finding the external answers because the processes are facilitated within your physical self. The healing in your body and soul, this light I am transmitting, fills you with guidance and connection to the source.

Mother earth and the spirits of your ancestors remind you this journey is all worth it, to experience the full spectrum of emotion and not dwell on what you've already let go of.

Say goodbye to the fear, even go as far as burying it into mother earth, whatever actions you are called towards to signify that you are making the permanent decision not to subscribe to fear. I stress something to physically represent that you are letting it go because the spiritual work requires the physical body to move forth the change.

Even the words "I release you" will completely transform your spirit. To let go and be able to fully open your heart to receive love and to share your gifts with humanity.

When you feel yourself holding onto that energy or emotion, forgive yourself and move on; it is never yours to hold onto. However, there might be a lesson in the experience itself.

Your love is everlasting, even at times when you've been consciously unaware of the power of your spirit. The work continues far beyond the words you receive in this transmission. This book is simply a conduit for remembrance. The real work starts with the application in your day-to-day life.

As you've clarified your soul contracts, you will continue to hold and create space for your fellow healers to do their work as you share your gifts in a community form because it is not a self-centric life; we are all connected. The work within the new earth in shifting the higher consciousness. You've held space for so long without even being conscious of it, lifting the universe's weight.

Chapter 11
The Truth Within

In the material world, there is no physical reciprocation of value. It is only the flow of energy in what you attract and create. So the intention is to sit with these energies as they show the way in.

Practice taking your attention off things or people in the external world, especially items of perceived value. This is one place where you will try to cling often. Instead, set material manifestations aside and contemplate how you want to impact the world.

You are returning to the present moment and disinvesting energy from predictable behavior patterns. The more you recall the past or try to shift toward material worries, you are drawn out of your center of power.

Just as drugs or alcohol can be a temporary numbing agent, those material or time-based concerns are taking you away from the present moment, therefore feeding unsupportive cycles of behavior.

When we go through trauma or adverse circumstances, we are not taught how to process those emotions. Therefore, when we run into challenges in the future, we have unconscious tendencies to engage in behavior that would otherwise be risky or not aligned with our truth.

If you've ever been led astray, allow this message to sit with you. Think about your daily life or behavior patterns that seem cyclical or anything that numbs you from the present moment. By taking inventory of these feelings, you have the awareness level embedded, which is all you need to release those negative patterns.

Your quantum field is full of possibilities. Rather than repeating negative things, you can transcend in the moment, even without meditation. This is done simply by sensing the color and depth of your energetic aura. In silence, tune into your intuition and imagine what colors of light you are surrounded by.

Rather than relying on spiritual tools or practices, you are learning to access this state of yourself in every moment.

The insignificant worries begin to fade away when you tune into your infinite frequency. It is really not up to you to be focused on the details of your daily life. Where the tendency is to plan or worry, lead with trust and knowingness. The connection to the divine in you will lead the way above all the chaos and challenges.

When your trust is unwavering, the universe will always over-deliver. There is an abundance of miracles for you to access at any moment. The importance of transcendence is to avoid getting stuck in the awareness phase. Being conscious is one thing, but being able to release emotions and patterning will take you beyond the normal range of perception.

It is misleading to define transcendence as surpassing others or being extraordinary because all humans have the same access to transcend beliefs and limitations. The overarching truth is that we are meant to move beyond such physical reality; our normal understanding has been conditioned previously to no fault of our own.

To achieve new heights of clarity and self-development, tune into what brings you into a peaceful state. If you think about the moments you wake up from sleep, this is one of the quietest spaces for your brain to expand.

While the tendency is to check the phone while still in bed or start thinking of the day to come, use this first moment of the day to go into a place of expansion. You are not attaching to worry or thoughts; this time is to allow yourself to be guided and receive information rather than becoming reactive based on the external inputs you are consuming.

Instead of looking for the comfort of the solstice in the external conditions or a way out, go within to explore the true nature and connection. Allow that connection to be a continuous flow of information that grows and expands.

I cannot stress enough the importance of finding a meditation style that works for you. That could be as simple as a movement-based practice or learning to find silence in the moment. If the traditional sitting of cross-legged seated meditation is hard to commit to, try other mindfulness techniques such as walking meditation, listening to healing frequencies, or guided meditation sessions. This is your time for connection, so propel yourself in ways you can consistently engage within.

The best place to do so is in nature, where you can harness a state of expansion through being outdoors much more accessible than when you are indoors. Opening the blinds and gazing outdoors into the sun can be powerful if the weather is not feasible.

Through daily walking meditation, I recommend the forest or a body of water; you will recognize that everything is home. Your home is always available in the Here and Now. Use travel, adventure, and play to upgrade your experience but remember that the true potential is already here for you to explore, no matter where you are.

As you commune with nature, the messages from your intuition will flow with ease, making way for more growth, inspiration, and creativity. This is a vital step, especially if you are easily overwhelmed because when the mind is racing, it seems more challenging to release the boundaries imposed by your physical reality.

As you develop your awareness and welcome more positive emotions, you will see the elevation of human consciousness from your own eyes. These peak experiences happen when you view the worries as a density of energy rather than a place you are staying in the physical body.

Instead of hitting a plateau or stagnancy by being weighed down by such concerns, the goal is consistently entering a state of peace. Your commitment is unwavering even when your mental and physical body feels challenged. Energy is a present exploration of life. Trust that god within you will lead the way.

Some people are called to share their stories, while others cloak themselves in silence. Regardless of the past levels or trauma to be shared, the truth may not be for the entire world to know, but they can learn from your experiences. This doesn't mean your face needs to be at the forefront of that sharing, but part of your mission is to raise the collective vibration. This is intended to be carried out between you and the messaging within.

It's funny how you create worlds in your mind, often for extended periods, without being conscious of it. As you absorb this channeled expansion of consciousness, you are finding the growth to embody simplicity, abundance, and joy. To create these worlds in alignment with your divine vision rather than it being a limiting barrier.

Understanding pleasure and joy involves a physical release component, especially when sexual trauma has been present. Think of somatic healing here. Instead of looking outside of yourself for validation or stimuli, which requires the action of doing, focus on expanding the fullness inside of you.

When you're alone, it can feel like you want someone or something to make that situation complete. But if everything is temporary and you are destined for miracles, would you choose to share your inner temple, or would you decide to have more discernment? The question is yours to explore, but introducing the practice of celibacy or energy selectivity will give you an entirely new view of things.

Many who understand the concept of dharma are enlightened through their earth connection. Dharma is going back to our true home. When we look deeply into ourselves, we realize that everyone and everything around us is our true home. There is nowhere to go physically, as that remembrance and purpose are within.

When our true nature or primordial essence is discovered, we understand ourselves and see that any other self has been imagined or believed. This pertains to putting on "masks" to appear ordinary or shame ourselves, while the true self is the experience of our lives where no suffering exists. Where we release all of that ego and surrender to infinite joy.

Take the lessons you've learned and leap into the quantum field of possibilities, as you are the fabric of creation. Continuously addressing situations no longer in your highest good will keep you in that zone of introspection. Cultivate positive energy to keep you focused on moving forward rather than falling back into beliefs of pain and suffering.

There is no reason to hold onto that sorrow or grief, as it is not meant to be buried inside. Learning to surrender is the art of letting go over and over again and feeling the true joy you are meant to experience. The beauty and interconnected web of infinite expression. As you are the one to expand this love and encouragement, it doesn't require faith from others.

I don't teach quick elimination of suffering because there is much to unlearn. It is possible to go into a rapid change, but the longevity factor may lead to further confusion or bondage. Instead of falling into denial or avoidance, it makes more sense to gradually dissolve these beliefs as they arise.

When you reach the cusp of a breakthrough, there is sometimes resistance before discovering the other side of creation. However, the opening process is far more enjoyable as the journey continues. We tend to attach far too much worry to the destination or the monetary value when those are just made-up constructs. Enjoy every bit of beauty along the way.

Your faith and role in the collective awakening should dictate where you are headed. This is where achievements have no barriers; the alignment and truth drive the expansion.

Nothing else really matters when you know the truth about what exists within. There is no more question of your purpose or what's next; having no clearly defined answer is okay. Because in every moment, your divinity exists, and the answers will be revealed as you tap into the forces of manifestation. It is the faith and courage you have to claim to unleash that power.

The home of spirit lives within you. You are touching your soul and feeling your aliveness simply by being in the present. By knowing our divinity, we can only look within the heart of true love. Within our internal hearts and through the love in all things.

We believe in the unity of All That Is but sometimes get lost in the mess of humanity or relationships, distracting when searching for something externally that can only be found internally. As our consciousness expands, we feel pressure. Pressure to change, pressure to grow, this pressure extends from our physical bodies to our external energetic bodies.

Union with another person is not a requirement. First, you must achieve this state of completeness within yourself before attracting a divine union. It is always challenging to differentiate what union is in your best interest, but having solid boundaries will help protect your energy. Listen to the voice within and follow that discernment.

When a person or relationship is in your path, it often reinforces a lesson of your strength. To show how important it is to trust the truth within you rather than being vulnerable to manipulation, lust, or other less-than-savory forces. The facts tend to be ignored when you seek comfort outside of yourself and ignore yourself to make another person feel good.

In many cases running to a false sense of comfort happens when you reflect on the side of yourself that needs to be healed. Through our earth connection, we find our true sensuality. Such sensuality comes from understanding and exploring the self, where you can explore connections with others from a place rooted in the totality of your desires.

Situations may present themselves as positive, and the intentions are inherently good, but what does your intuition say? The voice of reason must be your own, not what the other person is cleverly projecting. It is much easier to tell a story than to align with that projected truth.

Be the driver of your path and focus on what you know within your heart is in divine alignment. It may be good, but is it meant for your highest good? Continuing from a centered place here will lead you to quantum leaps. Those leaps exist when your attention is within.

Chapter 12
All That Is

I am attuning you through the voice of growth to enlighten you about All That Is. For you to truly comprehend and understand your inner world. Your inner world is the world you don't see physicality, where you exist in a race of unity, and judgment does not exist. The lessons you will learn in this place of expansion should be shared with others to transform their lives and activate their collective purpose on this earth.

If your faith is tested, your will prevails, and nothing will stop your actions from propelling forward. Faith is belief, and belief can be questioned without a solid foundation. Will power is rooted in you; it cannot be denied existence or watered down.

Being in this whole state of self-embodiment is where you are headed, which gives you the authenticity to expand into greater heights. Your higher self is essentially you being connected to the source of light, your divinely inspired self, where there is an understanding of your role in creation.

Feel the ease and expansion of your light. The key is to feel weightless and open in the physical body, not holding onto energy or blockages that no longer serve our best interests. Instead, we can be so bright and firm in our embodiment that our light spills out and radiates into others' energy fields.

This is the same reason other people may feel comfortable or absorb particular energies from being around you. Because they feel how you work with and embody your unique energy field, just as someone exudes confidence, those in full embodiment of their own energy will have a noticeable effect on others.

Take observation of this effect as it will drive self-awareness of your purpose. This is also a reminder to have energetic boundaries and not feel obligated to pour into others just because they want to be around your energy.

Affirm to yourself, "My presence is naturally beneficial. I am living inside out." You are not living in fear or suffering; instead, you are motivated by loving action. Creating your own unique affirmative prayers will bring you into that vibration of gratitude simply through the sound of your voice. Celebrate the spirit within you by using words to amplify your inner truth.

The more you're willing to turn within, the more you will be astounded by your greatness. In this transformation, the light expansion and awareness will be anchored. The experience of spirit is an invitation to go within.

Spend some time in deep meditation to develop that consciousness of how the spirit works through you. Because in those incoming moments of darkness, you can cultivate a new level of clarity.

Mastering yourself is coming into your source of truth, joy, and pleasure. The path to such mastery relies on exploring the true nature of the mind and All That Is. The material universe consists of many forms of life, matter, and energy, which reflect the outward manifestation of our inner being.

This activation opens the door for you to understand your inner temple and see the universe in its fully infinite nature. Reflect on where the resistance lies and, instead of attempting to shield yourself from pain or failure, be intent on accessing your full potential.

The most significant risk you have here is not growing but continuing down the path of least resistance that is leading nowhere. It might seem comfortable, but it hurts you to stay in that same old comfortable place.

It is your mission to bring light into this world. Cherish the fact that while this is a huge undertaking, you will feel empowered doing this work. The depths of darkness in your journey have accelerated the path to standing in your complete authenticity. For your vessel and voice are mastered as a vehicle for the work of the divine; to enlighten others and share this elevated conscious awareness. Even if you're not crystal clear on this mission at the moment, this activation will spark the unfolding process over time.

Reflect back on what you've learned during this initiation, and continue to welcome peace to wash over your vessel. Openness to continue absorbing the light and walking in the divine path. Your spirit is within you to guide you on your mission. Even when you may feel alone, the interconnectedness of self illuminates the way forward.

This is a constant source of compassion, kindness, and love. The vision is already evident, and it is not the direction we seek; it is the joy and fulfillment already rooted in the journey. There is a new definition of comfort to resonate with, not the comfort you desire or the complacency, but the self-love you experience. Giving you fullness in the experience of being home within and needing nothing while possessing the joy of everything.

A major part of self-mastery is no longer attaching to the energy that does not belong to us. This is where your clearing practices are vital to release and guard against unwanted attachments. Do clearing in the morning before your self-care to set a strong, centered foundation for the day.

Keep your protection in place and if you feel distracted or experiencing negative energies, disconnect from what's in front of you and clear the energies again.

The key is to identify the intrusive energies and cut them off midstream versus allowing them to continue cycling into a negative behavior. Don't fall for the temptation or allure, as your intuition can immediately tell the difference between something in your highest good and that which only appears to be.

You possess the strength to discern and stay within yourself. In this awareness, be grateful for the intelligence you always receive, not taking it for granted or ignoring your intuition.

Repeat this aloud as a reminder: "I am the light of the universe and forces of creation." Reminding and affirming this verbally in your own voice is a powerful course correction in alignment. Speak your prayers into existence and allow the forces to bring them into your reality. This is conscious creation, where you know what has been divinely sent. By receiving these gifts, there is no question whether they are for your highest good.

Bad energy and spirits will only keep pulling at you if you allow them to. When you protect yourself and say no with surety, they will not come into your energy field, no matter how much effort. It is up to your discernment to truly listen to your intuition of what is truly meant to support you versus what is trying to host off of you.

Setting these boundaries in all areas of your life means that the energy will flow much more beautifully, with ease and simplicity. Your strength radiates and helps to transmute all that is not for you to pure love.

Stop accepting and allowing things into your life based on the desires of others; rely only on your trust in the divine. This is not pointing you to follow a particular path. Instead, it is activating your inner faith.

Where the term God can have so many different names and beliefs associated, the truth of divinity within is already embedded in your consciousness. It isn't about labeling those forces from a place of ego or conditioning but knowing what it means to be one with that voice inside. Part of the ascension process and waking up spiritually is tuning into your existence's forces.

Listening to your source of the truth allows those messages to flow constantly. Not just when you sit in silence or pray but in all moments connected to this radiant light and the codes received from such.

If you ever find yourself questioning that or not feeling in tune with a message you receive, go outside and do some sun gazing. We are taught that the sun is damaging, but it contains endless codes of expansion and source energy. To serve as a reflection and brightness of the light and divinity within. The sun's rays never seem to look the same or shine in the same way, representing the truly infinite nature of reality.

Going outside or observing nature gives you a moment to tune in, even if the sun is not out. You can expand the self through natural means and begin to heal on a more profound level.

I've channeled these transmissions to help your inner reflections lead an endless journey of joy and peace.

To rid yourself of all the beliefs, fears, and perceptions that are not serving you. Instead of just reading these words, take the time to really sit with information and reflect on what it means through your own path.

Write down these reflections as they pertain to things that appear in your present reality. I stress this point as more than just the absorption of the knowingness but also the integration throughout the journey. The work is in how you apply this transmission and continue to integrate the messages within. The way that the transformation manifests in the current physical reality is meant for you to experience the abundance of love and fulfillment destined for you.

Chapter 13
Clarity Forward

The voice in your intuition is yours to access. It is your birthright to create more fullness and vibrancy simply by using the intention of creation. And through your place in this current illusion, you will remember the deep love for yourself and your connection to your ancestors.

As you ascend, remember the vibrations you carry and recognize where and when that vibration is triggered by external circumstances. Allow the feeling of safety to expand your confidence. Even in the presence of spirit can be inaction. Where genuine commitment requires unwavering courage to say no when needed to claim your personal peace.

The journey continues beyond setting boundaries and learning how to say no. Those are really the easy shifts; the difficulty lies in identifying your personal tendencies. So often, unconscious behaviors lead us down the wrong roads. It is time to reveal what you are avoiding.

The decisions we think are safe or comfortable sometimes open the door to more chaos. Sometimes the more attractive a situation seems, the more we are subject to being jaded away from our intuition and, ultimately, the truth. This is where more awareness needs to be cultivated.

Avoiding that uneasiness is as simple as being more conscious of our tendencies, such as loneliness or fear of being alone. As a root cause, where do these perceptions lead us to seek external validation? Think about the origin of those feelings, come to peace with them, and then release the weight. The key is to face that heaviness and look to the root.

Lean into the potential discomfort of being alone and learn to cherish the moments of inner reflection. These are the times that speak the most to our motives and values. Where do you feel drawn outside of yourself?

Even when seeking outside help, we must examine our motives. Is it from the need to be complete, or is there actual value in the connection? Is the perception of value influenced by what you see in the other person or what you know to be true?

This line of questioning will bring forward the accurate picture versus what someone else may want you to see. If it feels out of alignment, it is not for you. Don't ignore the signaling from your intuition, especially concerning a situation involving another person. Here you are creating energetic ties with a friendship or even a partner before listening to the voice of your intuition.

There are no external attachments or monetary values that matter in this lifetime. True abundance is knowing your magic, which naturally attracts everything you need and more.

To describe a soul whose consciousness leads to evolution is to describe the action they take, not the money they spend. Such illusions are created for you to put your attention in the wrong places.

Let me break that down, when you are focused on the material connection, you are going away from the trustworthy source of abundance. The god inside of you is walking out of the room, and you are focusing on an external construct from society. Yes, you need money to live, but the focus is not so much on getting the money as it is living every moment in alignment with the impact you are destined for. Such guidance comes within but creates a powerful domino effect for the collective consciousness of All That Is.

Returning to the home within yourself is recognizing how our thoughts manifest reality and attract frequencies in the external world. Achieving a state of mastery can be compared with control, except in this case, you surrender everything you thought you were to be in the essence and fullness of your spiritual self. At this point, you see that control was just an illusion.

When you think of that home as not a physical destination but remembrance and return, you can master your true self. The importance of this shift in perspective is the difference between living a mindless life controlled by ego and truly living to expand yourself beyond the depths of existence.

This is for you to be reminded that at any moment, you can use your breath to feel the highest frequency and connection inside. While it goes much deeper than just the breath, that is one way to put you into a centered state to embody that power.

By holding negative thoughts in your mind, your reality will reflect that with the people you meet and the circumstances you encounter. The outcomes will transform dramatically when you consistently show up for yourself and understand your connection to the world around you.

Being able to clear those weights, your consciousness transcends the perception of resistance. As a result, improvements happen quickly in the quantum field. Here you are aware of the positive charge that emotions such as gratitude and abundance hold.

Reflect on the triggers and behavior patterns that are repeating in your life. The goal is to grasp how your inner world interacts with what you attract and whether those circumstances are in your highest good or reflect negative emotions such as fear or shame.

It is almost as if we are accessing another world to get genuine answers. One that exists within the conscious mind, within the multitude of dimensions that we are present in. This is not the place for you to attempt to quantify the size of the astral universe or need to know every version or dimension of reality; it is an opening to manifest experiences and heights along the journey.

Beauty exists in the journey, where there is no valid destination you need to personify. The celebration is in the present moment and the potentiality that lives there. When our eyes are heavily focused on a goal or the next stage, the attention is dissipated to that future state.

If all of the miracles exist in the Here and Now, wouldn't that be the better place of focus and gratitude? Worry seems to fade away much easier when you find a piece of love or thankfulness, regardless of the current situation. It's like being wholly centered and keeping it centered versus worrying or placing fear toward future circumstances. Of course, setting intentions and goals are positive, but don't spend too long contemplating the future.

Find that surety in what you want, as the knowingness guides you to what is already meant for your life. The manifestation comes into reality when you stop fighting and receive only the destiny you've made space for and none of the excess noise.

Lean into that protected openness and show the universe you will continue to welcome new miracles. You are destined for so much more. In this activation, you are receiving a unique experience of life. To see from many lenses into the depths of your own soul.

It is less about the thoughts of the conscious brain and more focused on how you release attachment to weight or limitation. Where is your vibration now? What would it feel like to ease more into the moment and feel yourself expanding into higher dimensions?

Exist in the fullness of this moment and every moment that follows. You are learning to love yourself more and experience life from a lens of pure love. Step into your power and feel the essence and embodiment of your feminine and masculine aspects.

Maybe up to this point, you've felt what it feels like to be disempowered, hurt, or depressed in some form. The other perspective is feeling the pain or buried emotion and allowing that trauma to bring forth your desired growth. Ask yourself if you feel comfortable repeating the same destructive patterns that you've continued to allow in your life.

Coming into your power means defining what that embodiment will look like for your life. Use as much description as possible to think or journal what you feel when you are in your truth and feeling the love, abundance, and infinite expansion. This freedom is available to you every moment, and you can always choose to rewrite your story.

In fact, you were never meant to believe these lower vibrational frequencies, such as thoughts of not being enough or wanting to assert control over everything.

Just allow things to be. Whatever stage you are in, you have the power of creation to define the path forward. The more expansive and specific your vision, the clearer your direction will become. I am using words to create the space and container for you to do the work yourself.

These words will activate and guide you, but ultimately it is your free will to want a more meaningful and impactful version of life. This comes with the fact that cultivating a deeper awareness of oneself inherently gives you the power to be the author revealing the exploration of life. The key is in the introspection and connection to nature and self to access the knowledge beyond without the burdens of external distraction.

Everyone inherently possesses psychic traits, which may come in different forms, such as feeling, hearing, or seeing. It is easy for the messaging from the spirit world to come through in all forms when you remain open and centered in purpose. You are a vessel for divine expression. However, I was not always that way and had to look internally to listen to my intuition and not the nonsense outside.

I repeat these key themes as they are meant to be integrated as messages for your self-mastery applications. Be open to and receive as much as possible from meditations; even when in motion, you can find those moments to silence the mind and tap into source consciousness. For example, I enjoy walking meditations because I can tune into the sounds of movement and be in the energy of nature.

The more you work with different types of meditation, journaling, or channeling in general, the easier it gets to access such a state of expansion. Stop having expectations of where other people are at in their journeys, and just do the work for yourself. Focus on your experience.

Spend dedicated time with yourself, even if it's just 5 or 10 minutes a day, to sit there and really listen to how you are guided by your intuition. The voices will come through very clearly; it is just the level of trust that wavers.

You set the pace for your expansion as this is your path. I am a guide reminding you to set boundaries and protect your energy. You will be respected, and honestly, you should place no value on how others perceive things because we are all connected anyway.

Simply realizing the importance of boundaries will keep you grounded and in the zone of creation, rather than the subject of manipulation or just outright wasting energy. If what you are putting out there in a situation is not reciprocated, it's time to place more attention within rather than wondering why things didn't go your way.

Rather than avoiding the shadows of your previous vulnerability, you welcome the mirror of those shadow sides. Because we all have them, it is a matter of how well you will get to know yours.

How do we find evolution when the energy surrounding us is in misalignment? The physical sensation in your body tells us one thing about the limits placed on the mind. Meaning fear condemns ideas before they are even brought to fruition.

What exists beyond the limited perception is the truth of how we are multidimensional beings who are infinite by nature. To feel connected and live harmoniously, you must be aware of the energy you are emitting. Be willing to let go of those limiting beliefs and invite joy into your soul.

The principles of vibration describe the fundamentals of this process: where all things, both physical matter and energy, hold a specific vibration. The most basic form of such fractal matter is atoms, where science reveals that particles are always moving. So, as we exist, our bodies give off vibrations based on our emotional state. The key is to become conscious of the power to control those vibrations rather than allowing them to become dense energy weighing you down.

If there is stagnancy or you feel stuck in an area of your life, ask yourself where you are currently holding tension in the body. Bring attention to the sensations and then encourage free movement in those areas. For example, if you feel overwhelmed or stressed, you may carry tightness in the throat. This may indicate energy or emotion in that chakra energy center that needs to be released for you to speak and express your whole truth.

If you are avoiding the progression, don't sit and wonder why a blockage is present. The flow of energy we create unbinds the mystery surrounding our attention and the distractions that arise. If you seek to be fully conscious and aware of where your attention is placed, you will naturally vibrate from a more positive level.

Creation is the inner workings of your mind, where you are meant to bring new manifestations into the world. The goal of mastering self is to dig beneath the layers of societal imprinting to the truth and remembrance of your soul contracts. To break through internal barriers, you must seek to understand the root of your behavior.

When you come into a situation where things don't go as planned, think about how your vibration and thoughts played into that outcome. It may not always be the direct cause and effect, but since everything is connected, how could you be a cause? What is that situation mirroring from within you?

We tend to focus too much on reacting and get caught up in the emotion from the reaction rather than forging a more empowered path forward.

Find a place of silence with you to harness the effect you want on the world, and emanate the power and love you wish to attract.

Even what is presented and acted upon from the intent of love serves a greater purpose. Your genuine connection within only happens once you learn to silence your mind and listen. So, in the absence of chaos, a traumatized or troubled brain seeks comfort. Comfort exists inside.

Recalling the past or dwelling on unfavorable circumstances will continue to attract lower vibrational events. The universe within your mind can advance your well-being simply by seeking to grasp the truth of your spiritual nature.

Today I'm reminding you that you are more than enough. You are everything and deserve to feel the clarity I am embedding in your soul. Who you share your temple with affects your spiritual well-being, even starting with something as simple as the thought process surrounding those external situations.

About the Author

Meet Zoey Bullock, an inspiration leader, author and educational consultant who is passionate about empowering others to tap into their innate power and transform their lives. With over 12 years of experience teaching healing arts, she is known for her popular digital courses that inspire others to awaken their intuition.

Through her calling to the world of self-empowerment, Zoey experienced a number of profound healing journeys that forever changed the course of her life. This spiritual awakening led her to pursue the path of channeling messages from the ancestors and studying various healing modalities including energy work, meditation, and self-discovery practices.

In addition to her inspirational content, Zoey is a sought-after speaker and teacher, and has held space for others to heal online and in person through retreats and workshops across the globe. She is known for her warm energy, and her ability to connect others with their highest selves.

Zoey has become a trusted guide to activate higher consciousness in this shift to the new earth. Her mission is to empower others to live their best lives in a more connected, compassionate world. Since a young child, she has been connected to her inner wisdom and is now sharing her transmissions for others to access this birthright to awareness.

She's helped numerous clients, business owners and children to overcome limiting beliefs and cultivate awareness of their infinite self. Working with others from all walks of life gives her a humble perspective of healing and spiritual growth. Her writing and educational programs are both insightful and practical, offering actionable guidance and practices for self development.

Her intuitive and compassionate approach leads others back to their source of love and joy within. When she is not pouring into others, Zoey loves spending time in nature with her family. Her community continues to grow, contributing to important healing work particularly working with women who are healing from trauma and abuse.

She is a beacon of messages from the spirit world, shining light and clarity into the lives of many. Developing her own intuitive abilities has been a life-long journey that continues to bring miracles forth on a daily basis. Her heart is centered in the source of creation, continuing to share practices and music from the ancestors.

Through her best-selling books and courses, Zoey inspires others to overcome their limiting beliefs and live a life full of love, joy and abundance.